A Few Facts About

Buddhism

Emerging Perceptions in Buddhist Studies

1-2. An Encyclopaedia of Buddhist Deities, Demigods, Godlings, Saints & Demons — with Special Focus on Iconographic Attributes / by Fredrick W. Bunce. 2 Vols. ISBN 81-246-0020-1 (set)

3. Buddhism in Karnataka / by R.C. Hiremath; With a Foreword by H.H. The Dalai Lama. ISBN 81-246-0013-9

4-5. Pali Language and Literature: A Systematic Survey and Historical Study; by Kanai Lal Hazra. 2 Vols. ISBN 81-246-0004-X (set)

6. Maṇḍala and Landscape / by A.W. Macdonald ISBN 81-246-0060-0

7. The Future Buddha Maitreya: An Iconological Study / by Inchang Kim ISBN 81-246-0082-1

8. Absence of the Buddha Image in Early Buddhist Art / by Kanoko Tanaka ISBN 81-246-0090-2

Emerging Perceptions in Buddhist Studies, no. 9

A Few Facts About
Buddhism

Gunnar Gällmo

D.K. Printworld (P) Ltd.
NEW DELHI-110015

Cataloging in Publication Data — DK

Gällmo, Gunnar, 1946-

A few facts about Buddhism.

(Emerging perceptions in Buddhist studies, no. 9).

Includes bibliographical references (p.).

1. Buddhism. I. Title. II. Series: Emerging perceptions in Buddhist studies, no. 9.

ISBN 81-246-0099-6

First Published in India in 1998

Published in India by:

D.K. Printworld (P) Ltd.

Regd. office : '*Sri Kunj*' F-52, Bali Nagar

New Delhi-110015

Phones : (011) 545-3975, 546-6019; *Fax* : (011) 546-5926

E-mail: dkprint@4mis.com

Printed at : DP's Impressive Impressions, New Delhi-110059

Contents

Contents

1

Introduction

WHEN studying the three great world religions — Buddhism, Christianity, and Islam — it is important to make a distinction between teaching and tradition. All three were founded by historical persons. Thus, they each have an original doctrine. To know exactly what this original doctrine was may be difficult today, since neither the Buddha, Jesus, nor Mohammed left any written records when they passed away. Still, it is a fairly certain historical fact that such an original doctrine did exist.

This is a difference between founded religions on one hand and on the other hand ethnical religions, such as Judaism, Old Greek or Old Norse religion or Hinduism. The latter don't have a specific founder. They have grown spontaneously and without any kind of plan in a collective context. If an ethnical religion has at all got a more or less coherent doctrine, this has developed relatively late.

This book is dealing primarily with the Buddhist teaching, as far as we know anything about it through its oldest preserved texts, and only secondarily with tradition.

Buddhist terms often have two parallel and similar forms, one of which is in Pāli (a Middle Indian language closely related to the dialects probably used by the Buddha himself when teaching), and the other in Sanskrit (a standardized Old Indian, at the time of the Buddha and after it used only by learned circles). In the following text, the two forms have been separated by a slanting line (/), with the Pāli form before and the Sanskrit form after.

Sometimes you have to be careful with the Sanskrit form, since the same word may be used in Hinduism as well, but the same term does not necessarily mean the same thing in the two religions. In some essential aspects, Hindu and Buddhist thought are very far from each other. It is important not to confuse them, as done by many Westerners (and Hindus).

At the centre of Buddhism are the three Jewels: the Buddha (the Teacher), the *Dhamma/Dharma* (the Teaching) and the *Saṁgha* (the Community, the Fellowship, the Taught). Most important of these three is the middle one, the Teaching. As Buddhism sees it, the *Dhamma* is a method for getting to know reality such as it really is. The Buddha has his value as the person who has made the Teaching known at a certain historical time, but he is no prophet — Buddhism doesn't believe in revelation. The *Saṁgha* also has a great value, because it makes a mutual support possible between those who are walking the Buddhist path. The Buddha and the *Saṁgha* are historical phenomena, but the *Dhamma* is independent of history. The historical expression of the *Dhamma* is the *Sāsana/Śāsana*, which means 'message' (same as Greek *angelion* in *eu-angelion*, 'good message', the Latinized form of which in several languages means 'gospel'). The history of Buddhism is carried on by the *Saṁgha*, the Buddhist community in the widest sense to the word.

During the second night-watch he observed how other beings are dying and being reborn, and how they themselves determine the basic conditions of their own future by their intentional actions. Then he understood that this too was an area where he could spend the rest of his life observing more and more details, without getting anything done himself.

During the third night-watch he directed his attention to his own ignorance, that ignorance which is keeping us in the prison of conditioned existence. By bare attention he broke through this ignorance and attained perfect liberation: *nibbāna/ nirvāṇa.* By this, he became a Buddha.

At this point, it should perhaps be explained that the word *nibbāna* does not primarily mean some kind of post-mortal state. *Nibbāna* is quite simply perfect freedom from greed, hatred and delusion. It may also be good to explain, since this is a matter often misunderstood at least by Westerners, that a person who has reached *nibbāna* is not necessarily passive. Freedom from own desires does not mean indifference to needs of others.

[On the other hand, a being completely free from desire — which is the only kind of being which Buddhism would ever call perfect — would never even have the thought of creating new beings in order to glorify himself. Thus, an omnipotent creator god could not possibly be perfect, for his very exercise of omnipotence would be morally blameworthy. Exercise of power cannot be combined with perfect wisdom. Here is a fundamental difference between Buddhism on one hand and Judaism, Christianity, and Islam on the other.]

After his awakening, the Buddha spent seven weeks close to the tree under which he had sat. During this time, he was visited by two merchants, Tapussa och Bhallika, probably from Orissa in India (although the Buddhists of Burma insist that they came from their country). They gave the Buddha rice-

Siddhattha Gotama knew as much as he did, he offered to transfer the leadership of his movement to him.

But Siddhattha Gotama still wasn't satisfied. He couldn't find a teacher more advanced than the last one, so he decided to carry on alone. He wandered through Magadha, whose capital Rājagaha/Rājagṛha he had visited already as a young searcher, making a deep impression on king Bimbisāra (according to *Suttanipāta,* 3:1). At last he came to the place now known as Buddha Gayā, a short distance from the town of Gayā in the present Indian state of Bihar. There, he began practising some extreme yogic exercises, which attracted five other Samaṇas to join him. Finally, the harsh asceticism had exhausted all his strength, and he understood that self-mortification was a way as impracticable as had been the playboy life in the palace.

Now Siddhattha Gotama remembered (according to the *Majjhima Nikāya,* 36, 85, 100) how he once as a child, when his father was working, had sat down in the shadow of a tree and spontaneously entered a calm and concentrated meditation. Perhaps this might be a way?

Siddhattha Gotama began to eat as usual again, and the five ascetics were so disappointed with him that they left. Strengthened by the food, he now started meditating in a new way. What he had learnt from Āḷāra Kālāma and Uddaka Rāmaputta was concentration meditation, but now he used this concentration as a foundation for insight training: bare attention, without clinging even to meditative bliss.

During the first night-watch he remembered his former lives, with the help of his advanced concentration, as many as the time-span of those hours would permit. Then he understood that going on with this was no use, since the past has no first beginning, so he could have continued indefinitely.

to historical facts — he had stayed in the palace, he would according to the plans of his father have inherited the latter's position as a 'king' (or at least as a local big-shot), and for this task he would have been prepared in the worst possible way: by being kept isolated from ordinary people. Instead, he joined a way of life where his only hope of survival was receiving gifts from the villagers. This meant that he had to communicate with them. If he couldn't win their confidence, he would get no food.

One thing is clear about the great renunciation: Already at several places in the *Tipiṭaka* (*Majjhima Nikāya,* 26, 36, 85, 100), it is explicitly said that Siddhattha Gotama left home against the will of his parents, so he didn't exaggerate filial obedience — and this is another point where 'Buddhist' tradition often differ from Buddhist teaching. There are Chinese texts, where the Buddha is said to have admonished all children to obey their parents blindly; but if he had done so himself, there wouldn't be any Buddhism.

[In the same way, by the way, as there would hardly be any Christianity if Jesus had always done as Mary wished him to. One similarity between Buddhism and Christianity is the fact that both were founded by tramps.]

From this moment in the life of Siddhattha Gotama, the *Tipiṭaka* begins to give a richer biographical material. At several places (*Majjhima Nikāya,* 26, 36, 85, 100), it is told that he first went to see an old Samaṇa called Āḷāra Kālāma, and that he asked permission to live under his guidance. He was, and not long afterwards he had learnt everything that Āḷāra Kālāma could teach. The old man then proposed that they both would lead the other disciples, but Siddhattha Gotama wasn't satisfied. He proceeded to another Samaṇa called Uddaka Rāmaputta, who was slightly more advanced. There everything was repeated, and when Uddaka Rāmaputta learned that

Dalai Lama, who due to his exile is the first to be known in the West, actually seems wise enough not to be in very much of a hurry to get back to his throne.]

Because of this two-fold prediction it is said, in some legends almost entirely post-canonical, that Siddhattha Gotama's father did everything he could think of to ensure that his son would elect the way of power and not the one of wisdom. The *Tipiṭaka* mentions very shortly (*Aṅguttara Nikāya*, 3:38) that Siddhattha Gotama had a palace for each of India's three seasons: the winter, the summer, and the rains. In the Rains palace, he is said to have been surrounded by female servants only, and for the four months of that season never to have had to go down to the ground floor. During this time, according to post-canonical sources, he married at the age of sixteen, and got a son when he was almost thirty.

One legend, which has become very popular in Buddhist tradition (although hardly at all mentioned in the canonical texts), tells about four sights which made Siddhattha Gotama start thinking. In the *Tipiṭaka* (*Aṅguttara Nikāyā*, 3:38) is written only that he came to understand that, sooner or later, he would himself have to age, fall ill, and die. Later embellishments tell that at four occasions, or perhaps just one, he went for a ride in the palace gardens, or possibly outside — the details vary — and that he then saw first an old man, then an ill one, thereafter a corpse and finally a Samaṇa in perfect mental balance, whereupon his thoughts made him leave the palace and become a Samaṇa himself. This story has been retold many times, e.g., in Edwin Arnold's poem *Light of Asia* and in Bertolucci's film *Little Buddha.*

This 'great renunciation' may easily be misunderstood, if one doesn't remember the historical background. Siddhattha Gotama did not leave society. He did not avoid his responsibility. If—let's suppose that this legend is essentially corresponding

In great parts of Europe and Asia, this was the end of the Bronze Age and the beginning of the Iron Age. In the temperate zone at least, there was a marked change in climate with much lower temperatures. Perhaps this was one factor stimulating thought?

Besides, metals became widely used only when the Iron Age began. Bronze had been a luxury for the upper classes, so for others, the Bronze Age was actually just the last part of the Stone Age.

Certainly, this was a time of great changes.

The region where the Buddha lived and worked was called Majjhima Desa/Madhyama Deśa, which means 'Middle Country'. (Same as the Chinese call *their* country 'Middle Kingdom', and as some Western languages call the Mediterranean the 'Middle Sea'. We always love to put ourselves in the centre, don't we?)

Majjhima Desa was politically divided into several states. [Only during one single period of its history, all India has been united under one ruler — in London.] The two main ones were the kingdoms of Magadha and Kosala/Kośala. Society was pre-industrial and pre-capitalistic. Economically speaking, it was in transition from Slave Society to Feudalism.

Ideologically speaking, there was in north-eastern India at the time of the Buddha a polarization between two main currents. The right-wing, if I am permitted to express myself in modern terms, was Brāhmaṇism, dominated by a hereditary priesthood (the Brāhmaṇa caste) and officially founded on the Vedas. The left-wing was Samaṇism/Śramaṇism [please don't confuse with Shamanism, which is something completely different!], rejecting both caste and Veda. The Samaṇas/Śramaṇas were wandering ascetics, making use of the only way for dissidents in that society to be tolerated: to renounce all property, all family life and all possibilities of a public career, and seemingly to leave society.

Samaṇism consisted of several factions, with very little in common except their opposition against the establishment. Two of them have survived till our days: Jainism, which can be found almost only in India and among Indians abroad; and Buddhism, which disappeared from India about a thousand years ago, but only after getting a strong position in several neighbouring countries.

Although the Samaṇas did seem to leave society, they were not devoid of influence on social affairs in Majjhima Desa. Precisely in north-eastern India, the caste of warriors—Khattiya/ Kṣatriya—were, at the time of the Buddha, about as strong as the brāhmaṇas, and the two castes did not agree about which one should be regarded as superior to the other. In such a situation, the secular rulers — normally kṣatriyas — could support the Samaṇas to get a counter-balance to the brāhmaṇas' strong position in the spiritual pecking-order. Several leading Samaṇas, including the Buddha and the founder of Jainism, Mahāvīra, had also been born into Kṣatriya families.

Very little about Siddhattha Gotama's life before he became the Buddha is written in the earliest canonical text collection, the Pāli *Tipiṭaka* ('Triple Basket'). A lot more has been added by later legends, not least in the post-canonical Pāli literature.

It is often said that the Buddha's father, Suddhodana/ Śuddhodana, was a king. That is very much a matter of definition. The Pāli and Sanskrit word *rājā,* which is etymologically related to Latin *rex* (king), is not mentioned in connection with his name in the canonical texts, only in later ones. Perhaps he can be called a king in the same sense as the kings of the Iliad, who were actually just powerful and well-to-do farmers. Suddhodana's country, Sakya/Śākya, probably wasn't a quite sovereign state, but more or less dependent on the king of Kosala.

In the *Tipiṭaka* is just mentioned, very shortly, that Siddhattha Gotama had a very comfortable life at his parents' home, probably until he was almost thirty. It is said that his mother, Māyā, died when he was just one week old, and that he then was brought up by his mothers' sister Mahāpajāpati Gotamī/Mahāprajāpati Gautamī. [But nothing is said about parthenogenesis, that his mother should have been a virgin when giving birth to him. Some Westerners have tried to see such a case in some descriptions of the dreams that Māyā had at the time he was begot, about an elephant walking around her and entering her side, but they have probably projected a Christian way of thinking onto some Buddhist texts. The experience is described as a dream, not as waking reality. Besides Buddhism, although it does recommend some self-restraint, on the other hand does not glorify inexperience. It is said that Siddhattha Gotama himself had made a son the normal way, and it is hardly likely that his mother would have to be holier than he.] The delivery is said to have been perfectly painless and free of complications, although he was her first child, and although the childbirth is supposed to have taken place outdoors. [There are Westerners who have interpreted this to mean a Caesarian, but I think they have grossly exaggerated the level of that time's surgery. Local anaesthesia wasn't invented yet.]

In a poem in the *Tipiṭaka* (*Suttanipāta* 3:11) there is a story about the old Samaṇa Asita, whom the *deva*s told that the Buddha-to-be had just been born. [The word *deva* is often translated by 'god'. In a Buddhist context that is not very good, since *deva*s according to Buddhism can't be immortal, and are not supposed to be worshipped.] Asita now went to Sakya and asked permission to see the new-born child. He was very glad to know that Siddhattha Gotama would become a Buddha, but he wept when he understood that he himself was already too old to live to see that moment.

This story is of some historical interest, for it may — directly or indirectly — have been a model for two parts of Chapter 2 in St. Luke: the message of the angels to the shepherds, and Simeon's meeting with the child Jesus. It is also possible that both versions have borrowed material from even older tales.

[To many Christians and Muslims it might appear blasphemic to question the literal historical truth of a tale in the canon of one's own religion, but to Buddhists this is not very important, for Buddhism does not care quite as much about historical details. For Buddhism, what's really essential is the teaching as a method for one's own and other's liberation, not the historical circumstances around it. Buddhism doesn't demand that you believe in things that haven't been proved, and — unlike e.g. Christianity — it hasn't built its entire teaching on a number of historical assumptions. Belief in the letter of sacred texts is also alien to the spirit of Buddhism, which is fundamentally anti-fundamentalist.]

There is another legend that, when the Buddha-to-be was born, a number of Brāhmaṇas were brought together to predict his future. They said that he would become *either* a great ruler *or* perfectly enlightened; either a Lord or a Buddha, but not Lord Buddha, for that combination is impossible. This tells a lot about how original Buddhism looked at power: wise people don't want to rule, and those who do want to rule are not very wise.

[This is a point where Buddhist traditions have often deviated from Buddhist teaching. The most clear example of this is the Tibetan-Mongolian tradition, where historical causes have given rise to the Dalai Lama institution, demanding that one man be both spiritual guide — in both Tibet and Mongolia — and secular ruler — only in Tibet — and thus to combine two roles that even the Buddha couldn't. However, the present 14th

1

The Teacher (Buddha)

THE word 'Buddha' is not a name but a title, which could be translated by 'enlightened' or 'awakened'. [Since the English language is sometimes not quite clear, and since many Anglophone monolinguals — including some professional philosophers — have never learnt the difference between the concepts of logic and the conventions of language, it should be pointed out that, according to Buddhism, there is nobody who has enlightened or awakened him.] The historical person most often meant when the title is used, Siddhattha Gotama/ Siddhārtha Gautama, did not claim to be unique. Other Buddhas have existed before him, and others may still come.

Buddhism mentions three kinds of Buddhas:

1. *Sammasambuddha/Samyaksambuddha*, 'Rightly and Completely Awakened': A Buddha enlightened with no help from others at a time when the *Dhamma* is not known, and afterwards 'setting the Wheel of the *Dhamma* in motion', i. e., starting a Buddhistic teaching and founding a *Saṁgha* and a *Śāsana*, which are hoped to survive him. The word 'Buddha' without additions usually means such a one, and very often especially the historical Buddha of our age: Siddhattha Gotama.

2. *Paccekabuddha/Pratyekabuddha*, 'Private Buddha': This one, too, is enlightened with no help from others at a time when the

Dhamma is not known, but he does not 'set the Wheel of the *Dhamma* in motion'. A *Paccekabuddha* may give some elementary moral advise, but he is not capable of building up an organized *Śāsana.*

3. *Sāvakabuddha/Śrāvakabuddha,* 'Disciple Buddha': Enlightened at a time when the *Dhamma is* known, thus during a *Sāsana,* and with the support of a *Saṁgha.* That does not mean, however, that the *Saṁgha* is doing his job. He must take the decisive steps on his own.

The term *Arahant/Arhant,* 'Worthy One' (same meaning as Greek *axios* or Latin *dignus*), really is a synonym of *Buddha,* but mostly this third group is meant.

According to original Buddhism, all three have reached the same liberating insight. One difference between them is the circumstances under which they did it. Another is their pedagogical and organizational capacity.

Whoever has set up his mind to become a Buddha, especially if a *Sammasambuddha,* is called a *Bodhisatta/Bodhisattva.* (This is the original meaning of the word. It has been changed somewhat in later North Buddhist tradition.)

When the word 'Buddha' is used about a historical person, the one meant is Siddhattha Gotama/Siddhārtha Gautama. He lived about 2500 years ago in what is now Southern Nepal and north-eastern India. In Greece, the great philosophers would soon appear. In China, Lao-tzu and Kung Fu-tzu were probably more or less contemporary with the Buddha, same as Zoroaster (Zarathustra) in Persia. In Jewish history, the Babylonian Exile occurred about this era, with great consequences for the evolution of Jewish and Christian thought. [In the parts of the Bible written after the Exile, God is good and Satan evil. In its earlier parts, there is no devil — no, the snake in Genesis is *not* the devil, whatever you learnt at school — so God had to be both.]

cakes and honey, and then they became his first disciples by taking refuge in the Buddha and the *Dhamma*.

Now it is told (according to the *Vinaya Piṭaka, Mahāvagga, Khandhaka* 1) that the Freshman Buddha was pondering whether it would be any use trying to show to others the way which he himself had gone. That way was simple, certainly, but it wasn't easy. Its basic idea was to let go of all desire, all hatred, and all self-delusion — but what most people are living for are actually these three. Was there anyone at all who could understand what he was talking about?

These thoughts of the Buddha were perceived by the high *deva* Brahmā Sahampati. He had himself, during an earlier life as a human being, been a friar under the earlier Buddha Kassapa/Kaśyapa (according to the *Saṁyutta Nikāya* 11:8:57). Now he was scared at the thought that the Buddha's knowledge would pass away with him, for this would be a disaster for the worlds. Therefore he descended from his own world, appeared to the Buddha, and pointed out to him that, in spite of everything, not *quite* all people were *completely* incapable of understanding. There were some 'with but little dust on their eyes'. They would be helped if the Buddha started teaching, but if not, they might have very great difficulties. That argument made the Buddha agree to begin his activities as a teacher and organizer.

[Please note that I won't, in the English version of this book, talk about 'Buddhist monks'. A member of a *cloistered* monastic order, e.g., the Benedictines, is a monk. A member of an *open* monastic order, e.g., the Franciscans, is not a monk but a friar. The Buddhist monastic *Saṁgha* is so open it shouldn't even be called an order, so neither term is quite to the point, but 'friar' is less wrong then 'monk'. Many languages don't have a good way of expressing this distinction, but English does, so I see no reason not to use it.

Still less will I talk about 'Buddhist priests'. A priest is an administrator of sacraments, which in Buddhism exist only in some later schools, such as the Tibetan one.]

Whether you wish to believe in the letter of this tale or not is, from a Buddhistic point of view, not very important. It's the same with some tales who can be found already in the *Tipiṭaka*, and in even more detail in later texts, about how Māra — the tempter in Buddhist tradition — is trying in all ways possible to prevent Siddhattha Gotama from becoming a Buddha. The essential thing is not whether Māra and Brahmā are actually existing beings in their own right or not. What's important is the psychological meaning: Māra as the powers, personal or impersonal, within or without ourselves, who are always trying to stop us from doing the right things, and Brahmā as (in this context) the higher perspective which makes sure that we are not getting stuck in a too narrow outlook. [There are other tales, already in the canon, where Brahmā instead, as a joke with the belief in an omnipotent creator god, is described as a very powerful but rather stupid being who *believes* himself to have created the world, but who is badly mistaken about this.]

Now the Buddha thought about whom to begin with. First he thought of his own old teachers, Āḷāra Kālāma and Uddaka Rāmaputta, but that turned out to be too late. The first had died one week ago, and the other did it last night.

Then the Buddha came to think of the five Samaṇas, who had joined him when he struggled and sweated with his ascetic exercises. Afterwards, they had left him, and now they were at a place nowadays known as Sārnāth, just outside Benares, in a deer park. Today, you can go from Gayā to Benares (or Vārāṇasī, as it is officially called) in a few hours by train, but this happened a couple of millennia before the first railways, so the Buddha had to walk. This, by the way, was his normal way of travelling. Horses were rare in India, and ox-carts weren't much faster than his own feet.

Both Buddha Gayā and Sārnāth are today important places of Buddhist pilgrimage. In Buddha Gayā the Buddha was born (although the Buddha-to-be, Siddhattha Gotama, was born 35 years earlier in Lumbinī in present Nepal), and in Sārnāth the *Saṁgha* was founded.

It is said that his awakening occurred at the full-moon day of May, and according to South Buddhist tradition both the birth of the Buddha-to-be and the death of the Buddha also happened on this full-moon day.

Three months later, i.e., at the full-moon day of July, just when the rains were about to begin, the Buddha met the five Samaṇas. These decided to show their displeasure with his 'luxury life' by not rising to him or receiving his alms-bowl and outer robe. They should only prepare a seat for him, if perchance he would like to sit down. But when he approached, they were not able to do as they had just decided. Later, when they talked to each other, they noticed that he didn't express himself the same way that he had done before. Finally he gave them his first sermon, known as the Benares Sermon (*Dhammacakkappavattana Sutta*), about the Four Noble Truths: unsatisfactoriness, the cause of unsatisfactoriness, the end of unsatisfactoriness, and the way to the end of unsatisfactoriness.

According to a tradition hinted at in the *Suttanipāta*, the five ascetics were not the only listeners at this occasion. Two demons (*yakkha/yakṣa*) are also said to have been present, as a sign that the teaching of the Buddha is not meant only for those who are very pious already.

When the sermon was finished, one of the five Samaṇas is said to have reached the point of no return on his way towards awakening, the so-called Stream Entry, and become what is named a *Sotapanna/Śrotapanna*. Somewhat later, the same thing is said to have happened to the other four.

In his second sermon (*Anattalakkhana Sutta*), which was also given to the five Samaṇas soon after the first one, the Buddha expounded one of the most central thoughts in his teaching: the non-existence of a permanent ego. When this sermon was finished, all the five ascetics had become *arahants*, so now there were six of them in the world.

Not a very strong beginning, it might seem, but now at least there finally was a *Saṁgha,* in two meanings of that word: a community of friars (*bhikkhusaṁgha/bhikṣusaṁgha*), as the Buddha had just accepted the five as such, and a community of noble ones (*ariyasaṁgha/āryasaṁgha*), i.e., of people gone far enough to be either awakened, or at least sure of becoming so. Since that moment, it is customary for Buddhists to take not only two refuges, as Tapussa and Bhallika had done, but three: in the Buddha, the *Dhamma,* and the *Saṁgha.*

[Buddhists of the Tibetan tradition have added a fourth refuge, to the personal teacher, and they recite it even before the three original ones. This fourth refuge was never recommended by the Buddha, and it reflects a *guru* worship that is really more Samaṇist and Hindu than Buddhist.]

The little community soon started to grow. It is told (according to the *Vinaya Piṭaka, Mahāvagga, Khandhaka* 1) that there was a rich man named Yasa, son of a wealthy merchant, and that he owned —just as Siddhattha Gotama had done before he ran away from home — one palace each for the winter, the summer, and the rains; that in the Rains palace he was surrounded by female servants only, and that during all of the rainy season, he never to have had to go down to the ground floor. [This kind of stereotyped repetitions of certain sections is a good reason not to believe unconditionally in all the historical details mentioned in these texts. The existence of these repetitions is probably due to the fact that the *Tipiṭaka* was an oral literature to begin with, learned by heart during several generations before written down.]

Regarding Yasa, there are also told some more details which a later tradition has ascribed to Prince Siddhattha too, although the *Tipiṭaka* doesn't say anything about it, namely that he once, when entertained by the women around him, happened to fall asleep while it was still early, and that his servants then followed his example. But a night lamp was burning, and when Yasa woke up before the others, he happened to see what they looked like when asleep, and that wasn't a very pretty sight.

So Yasa got fed up with it all, put on his gold slippers and left his home and the town. This happened during the Buddha's first rainy season, while he was staying in the deer park outside Benares, and that was where Yasa went. The Buddha had risen early and was pacing up and down in meditation. When he saw Yasa coming, he sat down on his own seat, and there he received him.

When Yasa arrived he exclaimed, still full of his impressions from the palace: 'This is horrible!' 'No, it isn't', the Buddha replied. 'Please sit down! I'll teach you the *Dhamma.*'

So Yasa did, and the Buddha started teaching him in the way he would later always do, when talking to people less well prepared than the five Sāmanas had been. He didn't take up the Four Noble Truths at once. Instead, he elected a gradual approach. First he talked — 500 years before the Sermon on the Mount — about the importance of giving and of living a moral life, and about the bliss to which that can lead. But then he went on — unlike the Sermon on the Mount — to warn that no bliss is eternal, and that whoever wants to be completely free will sooner or later have to renounce both heaven and hell. Then, when he saw that Yasa was prepared, open, free from hindrances, eager to learn and full of confidence, he finally explained to him the Four Noble Truths — the teaching peculiar to Buddhism. Then Yasa became a *sotapanna.*

In the meantime, back at the palace, Yasa's parents had

risen and found their son disappeared. They sent out messengers in all directions, and Yasa's father went to the deer park at Sārnāth. The Buddha hid Yasa for a while, so his father couldn't see him, and then he taught the father in the same way that he had done with Yasa earlier. When this sermon was done, the father had become a *sotapanna*, and Yasa himself an *arahant*; so now there were seven *arahants* in the world. Yasa also became the sixth Buddhist friar in this *śāsana*, and his father became the first Buddhist layman to take all three refuges (Tapussa and Bhallika having been able to take only two, since they became laymen before the *saṁgha* was founded).

Yasa's father now understood that it wasn't a very great idea to have his son return to his family. Instead he contented himself with inviting the Buddha and Yasa to have lunch at his palace the same day. Before food was served, the Buddha taught Yasa's mother and former wife. They too became *sotapanna*s, and the two first Buddhist laywomen of this *sāsana*.

Four friends of Yasa's, living in Benares and belonging to leading merchant families, also joined the new *saṁgha* and attained the highest goal. Now there were eleven *arahant*s in the world. The same thing happened to fifty other friends, bringing the total number of *arahant*s to 61.

[When you find numbers of two or more digits in an Indian text, you have good reasons not to believe in it too literally. Both rounding off and exaggerations are part and parcel of South Asian literary tradition, and there are certain codes like 'five hundred' for 'many', or 'eighty thousand' for 'many, many'.]

The Buddha had met the five Samaṇas about the time when the rains began, and as long as they went on it wasn't much use wandering about, as everyone will understand who has experienced a tropical rain. [In Buddhist tradition, as well as in the traditions of other religions, it has been a common thing to go on year after year, century after century, applying certain rules rigourously without realising that they were made under specific circumstances. Even today, all friars of the South Buddhist tradition are principally forbidden to travel during the rains — i.e., during those months, from July till October or November, when it was raining where the Buddha was living, even if they themselves live at places where the rains occur at other times, or even in temperate zones where there isn't any rainy season at all.]

After the rains, the Buddha gave to the sixty-first friars a sermon that has often been compared to the Christian command to mission of Matthew, 28:18-20. I think this is a great mistake. The latter said that, because 'all power is given unto me in heaven and in earth', the apostles should 'teach all nations' (King James Version) or, even worse, 'make all nations my disciples' (New English Bible) or 'make disciples of all nations' (New Revised Standard Version). (The two later translations are probably more correct than King James. The source text has *mathēteúsate pánta tà éthnē.*) The Buddha said nothing about power, and he wasn't megalomanic enough to try to 'teach all nations', or callous enough of others' integrity to 'make all nations my disciples'. Instead he told the friars to wander and to proclaim the *Dhamma* 'for the welfare and happiness of many, out of compassion for the world, for the benefit, welfare and happiness of *devas* and men' (Ñāṇamoli's translation, with the word 'gods' replaced by '*devas*'). The Christian call is motivated by subservience to an Almighty God, but the Buddha's invitation is built on compassion with those who are to receive the message. Christ wants (according to this text) to convert the nations, while the Buddha wishes to help individual persons. Not 'all', just 'many', knowing how impossible it is to teach anything to those who don't want to learn.

[It should be admitted that there are today Christian people who interpret their own call as if it actually were the Buddhist one, but in the history of Christianity such a tolerance has insofar been common only when Church was weak. It should also be kept in mind that Christ, according to the Bible, is said to have pronounced these words only after his death and alleged resurrection. Since that resurrection has never been proved, and since people normally don't talk very much after death, it is very probable he never said it.]

In any case, the sixty friars went out, and evidently the time was ripe, for they got in touch with many who were interested, and there were quite a lot who wished to become Buddhist friars themselves. The increasing number of friars, and the varying level of the freshmen's wisdom, to say the least, made it necessary to make rules for the growing monastic community, and to decentralize the right to ordain new friars. (For the laypeople, there were just some elementary rules of morality.)

India at this time had absolutely no tradition of democracy, and it was costumary for the founder of a religious community to decide alone about its rules. So the Buddha did as well, as long as he lived, but unlike most other *Samaṇas*, he was clever enough to plan an organization which would make it possible for the Buddhist community to survive him by, until now, 2500 years. Interestingly enough, he refused to appoint a successor to the leadership of the community, and decided that the *saṁgha* of friars should be managed after his death in a way that have to be called democratic, probably sometime before the ancient Greek launched that term. By this, the Buddha actually founded the world's first known international popular movement.

The tradition of Zen, which arose in East Asia about one thousand years after the Buddha, is claiming that the friar Kassapa/Kaśyapa, regarded by that tradition as its first patriarch, had been appointed by the Buddha as his successor, to lead the *Saṁgha* after his death; but such a view has no support in the oldest sources. What Kassapa did, according to these, was to convene, after the Buddha's death but at his own initiative, a council to edit the Buddha's memorized sermons and the disciplinary rules of the friars — orally, for writing wasn't very widespread. (At this time, it was used mainly for economical book-keeping.)

The fact that Kassapa managed to do this was largely the merit of the Buddha's cousin Ānanda. During the first twenty years of the Buddha's work, different friars used to take turns to help him with some practical details, but finally this system got too complicated, so the Buddha preferred to have one single friar take care of the matter. Ānanda was offered the position, and he accepted on one condition: each time the Buddha gave a sermon, Ānanda should either be present or have it repeated to him afterwards by the Buddha. Ānanda's auditory memory was extremely good, so he became a kind of living library of the Buddha's teaching.

It is told that Ānanda was so busy taking care of the Buddha, and learning all his sermons by heart, that his work on his own development was delayed, and he didn't become an *arahant* as long as the Buddha was alive, only the very night before the beginning of the First Council. [Some authors — such as F. Harold Smith in his book *The Buddhist Way of Life* — has taken this to mean that Ānanda wasn't a friar but a layman, but that is a misunderstanding.]

Many Western authors have called Ānanda 'the Buddha's favourite disciple', but as far as I know there is no such expression in the *Tipiṭaka*, and I think it is fundamentally alien to Buddhist thought for an *arahant* to keep favourites. The thought has probably arisen as an over-hasty analogy with the Gospel of St. John, where John the Evangelist is consistently calling John the Apostle 'the disciple, whom Jesus loved' (perhaps because John the Evangelist *was* John the Apostle, and didn't want to write his own name, or because he at least wished the reader to believe so).

With all due deference to Ānanda — he may be said to have played the same role in Buddhist tradition as the evangelists did in the Christian one, since he is said to have if not written, then at least preserved orally a lot of the canonical texts — still, two other friars are regarded as foremost in the *saṁgha* at the time of the Buddha: Sāriputta and Moggallāna (or Śāriputra and Maudgalyāyana, if you prefer the Sanskrit forms of their names). Their story is one example — in addition to the one of the Buddha himself — that original Buddhism did *not* mean (unlike many branches of Hinduism, and even many later traditions of Buddhism itself) that a personal teacher is absolutely indispensable to attain the highest goal. They are said to have become *sotapannas* already before meeting the Buddha — Sāriputta having heard one of the five ascetics, named Assaji, recite a four-line stanza, and Moggallāna when he had heard Sāriputta repeat the same stanza; and it is said to be impossible for a *sotapanna* not to become an *arahant* sooner or later.

This is how it happened (according to the *Vinaya Piṭaka, Mahāvagga, Khandhaka* 1):

Near Rājagaha, then capital of Magadha, lived a *samaṇa* named Sañjaya with a large number of disciples, 250 to be exact. Two of them were Sāriputta and Moggallāna. They had agreed that if one of them did attain the highest goal, he would tell the other.

The Buddha too was living outside Rājagaha at the time, together with Assaji and some other disciples. Assaji was one of the five ascetics to whom the Buddha had given his first sermon. One morning he arose, dressed, took his bowl and went into Rājagaha for alms, according to the custom of *samaṇas* at that time. When Sāriputta saw him, he was deeply impressed by Assaji's graceful movements, and he understood that this friar must be an *arahant.* Therefore he followed him, and when Assaji had finished his alms-round, Sāriputta went up to him, and they exchanged the usual polite phrases. Then he asked him what teacher he had, and what teaching he was practising.

Assaji explained who the Buddha was, but he said that he was too new in the *Dhamma* to be able to expound it in detail. Sāriputta then asked for a short summary, and Assaji said:

> "The Perfect One has told the cause
> Of causally arisen things;
> And what brings their cessation, too:
> Such is the doctrine preached by the Great Monk."
>
> (Ñānamoli's translation. 'Monk' is not quite correct, as I have noted above. 'Friar' would be better, or '*samaṇa*', as is the world in the Pāli original.)

When Sāriputta heard this, he at once became a *sotapanna.* Later, when he met Moggallāna, the latter was as impressed by Sāriputta's behaviour as he himself had been by Assaji's, so he understood that something must have happened. As soon as Sāriputta had read Assaji's stanza, Moggallāna too became a *sotapanna.* The two decided to visit the Buddha as soon as possibly, but before that they would inform their brethren in Sañjaya's community. All the 250 decided to accompany them, but Sañjaya himself got sore at losing face like that, so he stayed. According to the text, he got so angry that hot blood gushed from his mouth. This is a common phrase in the *Tipiṭaka* about competing teachers who have been worsted, and it probably means that he died of his own rage. (In a later case—the founder of Jainism, Mahāvīra, or Nigantha Nātaputta as he is called in the Pāli texts — the competing doctrine has survived in India till our days, but the Jains themselves have, for some reason, a quite different opinion about Mahāvīra's way of passing away. Luckily, the Buddha himself has, according to the *Tipiṭaka*, advised us not to believe blindly in any *Piṭaka*.)

When the Buddha saw Sāriputta and Moggallāna approaching, together with the 250 *samaṇas*, he told the friars around him that the two would become the foremost members of the *saṁgha*, and when they asked to be accepted as friars, they were at once ordained by a few words of the Buddha. Moggallāna became an *arahant* after one week, and Sāriputta after two.

One interesting detail about Moggallāna is seldom mentioned, but it does illustrate the difference between Buddhist and Christian/Muslim notions of evil. According to the *Majjhima Nikāya*, Moggallāna at one occasion was tempted by Māra, who tried to disturb him; but Moggallāna is then said to have kindly informed Māra that he wasn't very easily fooled, for once in an earlier life *he had himself been Māra*, and for all the bad things he did at that time, he afterwards had to boil in hell during eighty thousand years, and that wasn't nice at all; so little Māra had better, for his own good, to devote his energies to something else.

The meaning of this is that, according to Buddhism, no divine or diabolic positions are eternal. If there is a Māra or a Brahmā, a Satan or a Yāhweh, then the present holder has his office for a certain time, and then someone else will take over. Several religions believe in a god who is existing by himself without having arisen due to certain causes, a god that just is who he is without having come into being and without having ever to pass out of being; but Buddhism sees no reason for such a belief. The story also tells us that no infernal punishments are eternal and, above all, that no evil is incurable. Even if you have been Old Nick himself in a past life, you may become a chief disciple of a Buddha in a future one — but first you must smart for what you did.

Both Sāriputta and Moggallāna died just before the Buddha. Sāriputta died of an illness, but Moggallāna was brutally murdered.

Another friar, who just as Ānanda was a cousin of the Buddha's, was named Devadatta. The two are even said to have been ordained at the same occasion (according to the *Vinaya Piṭaka, Cullavagga, Khandhaka* 7).

Devadatta is the bad guy in Buddhism's canonical texts, and it isn't impossible that he may be the literary model for Judas Iscariot in the Christian gospels. According to the text cited above, he is told to have offered the Buddha to take over the leadership of the community of friars himself, as the Buddha was so old and tired. The Buddha, who, unlike some of his followers in our time, did not exaggerate his politeness, answered that he couldn't even think of handing over the community to Sāriputta and Moggallāna, so much less than to 'a clot of spittle like you'. Then the Buddha made a public declaration that Devadatta, who until then had been met with great respect, no longer was the same person as he had been and that neither the Buddha nor the *Dhamma* nor the *saṁgha* should henceforward be judged after Devadatta's devices. Nobody but Devadatta himself would be responsible for his actions.

And that was a pretty good decision, for at about the same time, Devadatta agreed with the crown prince of Magadha, Ajātasattu/Ajātaśatru, that the two would kill both the Buddha and Ajātasattu's father, king Bimbisāra, so Ajātasattu could be the king and Devadatta could be the Buddha. This plan didn't succeed very well. Ajātasattu had a go at killing his father, but was caught and arrested by the latter's bodyguards.

Neither did Devadatta manage to kill the Buddha, although he tried repeatedly.

When Bimbisāra was informed, he pardoned Ajātasattu, voluntarily abdicated and transferred his power to him. The Buddha, however, did not agree to transfer his authority to Devadatta. The latter then tried to cause a schism in the *saṁgha* by adding to the training rules of the friars, already rather strict, five more: that all friars should live in the jungle and not close to a village; that all friars should eat only the food they got in their alms-bowls and not accept lunch invitations; that all friars should sew their clothes of thrown-away rags and not receive ready-made robes; that all friars should live under trees and not under roofs; and that all friars should abstain from eating meat or fish. As Devadatta knew perfectly well that he would, the Buddha refused to accept these demands. Whoever wished to live according to such rules could do so, but making them compulsory was out of the question. Devadatta then informed the public that he, at least, wasn't as lax as the Buddha. In a country like India, with very strong traditions of asceticism, this made a deep impression.

[These facts are good to know when later Buddhist teachers, e.g., the American 'Zen Master' Philip Kapleau, claim that every true Buddhist must be a vegetarian. According to the oldest sources, the Buddha himself was of a different opinion.]

Devadatta now took 500 (i.e., many) friars with him, broke away from the Buddhist *saṁgha* and founded one of his own, with himself as a leader and with the five new rules added to the common ones. His triumph was short, however. The Buddha sent Sāriputta and Moggallāna to him. They arrived when he was busy teaching his disciples. Devadatta welcomed them, believing they had converted to his party. After a while he felt tired, asked Sāriputta and Moggallāna to continue the lecture, lay down, and slept.

Sāriputta and Moggallāna did as Devadatta had asked them, and so efficiently that all the friars became *sotapannas*; and that was the end of their respect for Devadatta, for he wasn't one. They all went back to the Buddha, and when Devadatta woke up he was so furious 'that hot blood gushed from his mouth'.

The *Tipiṭaka* doesn't say more about Devadatta's end, but the medieval commentary adds that the earth opened up and that he dropped straight down into hell, there to abide until the end of this age. The commentary also tells us that Ajātasattu, having ascended his throne, first had his father imprisoned and then murdered, but the *Tipiṭaka* is silent about this as well.

Power is corrupting, and much wants more. To Ajātasattu, ruling his own country Magadha wasn't enough. According to the *Saṁyutta Nikāya* 3:14-15 he started, not very successfully, a war of aggression against the neighbouring country of Kosala, where king Pasenadi/Prasenajit was a lay follower of the Buddha, just as Ajātasattu's father. Pasenadi was also Ajātasattu's maternal uncle.

According to the medieval commentary (the *Tipiṭaka* says nothing of the matter), Pasenadi too was dethroned by his own son. He then decided to flee to Magadha and ask for Ajātasattu's help. (It seems that political alliances could shift very fast already at that time.) When he arrived at Rājagaha, the city gates were already closed for the day, so he had to spend the night in a simple hovel outside the city wall. During the journey, he had not been very careful about his food. He got some kind of food poisoning, and in that night he died.

Finally, after the Buddha's death, Magadha annexed Kośala. That was the beginning of an empire which, a couple of centuries later, would include most of India.

The fact that Buddhism's canonical texts speak so much

about friars may have a connection to the fact that it was the community of friars that preserved these texts, first orally for some centuries, and later also in handwriting — secular scholarship didn't get much access to them until the nineteenth century, and only then they started to be printed. But the Buddha gathered around himself not only friars. Not even only friars and laypeople, but also friaresses (often called 'nuns', although this word is as wrong in a Buddhist context as 'monks') — and this was a revolutionary thing in that environment. As far as we know, the Buddhist community of friaresses was the first female group of this kind.

In the *Tipiṭaka* there is a book, the *Therīgāthā*, with poems only by friaresses. As far as I know, this is the first all-female literary anthology in recorded history.

This is what is said to have happened, when the *bhikkhunisaṁgha/bhikṣuṇīsaṁgha*, the Buddhist community of friaresses, was founded:

It is told (according to the *Vinaya Piṭaka, Cullavagga, Khandhaka* 10) that the Buddha once was living in his old country, Sakya. His maternal aunt Mahāpajāpati Gotamī/ Mahāprajāpati Gautamī had, during his childhood, taken care of him after the death of his mother. Now she came to him and asked him to ordain women too. This was something unheard of at the time, and at first the Buddha refused — probably not out of disrespect for women, but because he understood what complications this would cause in the relation of the Buddhist community to the society around them (in addition the those problems which use to arise when boy meets girl).

But Gotamī had a strong will, and she wouldn't give up quite as easy. She and some lady friends of hers just shaved their heads and dressed in the same kind of robes that was used by the friars, and because the Buddha had in the meantime left Sakya and gone to the town of Vesālī/Vaiśalī, they walked there. When they arrived, they met Ānanda, who asked them what they wanted and promised to take the matter up with the Buddha.

The Buddha first gave Ānanda the same answer as he had given to Gotamī. Then Ānanda asked the Buddha if women too, if they would live the same kind of life as the friars anyway, would be able to go as far as these could. The Buddha had to answer yes. There was no difference between the sexes regarding such capacity.

Then Ānanda pointed out everything that Gotamī had done for the Buddha-to-be in the place of his mother, and when confronted with such a debt of gratitude, the Buddha couldn't go on refusing. However, he made more practical demands on the friaresses than on the friars, probably because he was more realist than fundamentalist, and because a complete equality between the sexes, then and there, could have provoked persecutions from the non-Buddhist people around them; and also because he cared for the security of the friaresses themselves. [At first, he demanded the friaresses should not spend the rains at a place with no friars; and later, when a female *arahant* had been raped, that a friaress shouldn't live alone under any circumstances. I have heard that even today, it is not advisable to send a nurse alone to an Indian village. . .]

In South Buddhist tradition, the *bhikkhunīsaṁgha* died out about a thousand years ago, due to some formal shortcomings in the ordination. In China it has continued till our days, though, and there is a discussion going on whether it would be possible to revive it in the South as well. The 'nuns' existing today in Ceylon, Burma, and Siam (or Sri Lanka, Myanmar, and Thailand, as their respective governments have renamed them) are strictly speaking laywomen who have adopted some extra training rules.

It is a common misconception that Buddhism is really meant

only for friars and friaresses; but if the Buddha had wished that, he would hardly have organized his community in the way he did. You see, he took over the common custom of Samaṇas not to have paid jobs. His friars should live of gifts from the laypeople.

[Some people have been shocked by this, especially if they live in countries with a fairly high degree of employment. People in countries with a high *un*employment, such as India had at the time and still has, may understand it easier. In e.g., Japan, where the problem often has been a lack of workers rather than a surplus, the organization of the Buddhist community has also been quite different.]

Neither were the friars permitted to actively beg for food. They should just receive what was given to them, without any pressure. Thus, economical power in the oldest Buddhist community was exclusively placed with the laity.

Neither is it true, as has been said in many books, that only friars (and friaresses) could, according to the Buddha, reach the highest awakening. In the *Tipiṭaka* are mentioned some lay *arahant*s, and many lay *sotapanna*s; and as a *sotapanna* is certain to become an *arahant* sooner or later, it is the *sotapanna* level rather than the *arahant* one that should be compared to what some other religions call 'salvation'.

The two first Buddhists, Tapussa and Bhallika, were laymen, as has already been mentioned. A layman of special importance to the Buddha was his 'private doctor' Jīvaka. Another was the rich merchant Anāthapiṇḍika/Anāthapiṇḍada, who donated to the Buddhist community a property called Jetavana, near Kosala's capital Sāvatthi/Śrāvastī. There the Buddha spent most of his rainy seasons.

During the last year of the Buddha's life, according to the *Mahā Parinibbāna Sutta* of the *Dīgha Nikāya*, king Ajātasattu of Magadha had the idea to annex the neighbouring republic of

Vajji. He knew that the Buddha was a clever man, but perhaps he had not quite understood in what way he was clever, so he sent one of his ministers to him, when the Buddha was staying close to his capital, to get some advice about how to go about it in order to succeed.

Now the Buddha was no great friend of expansionist politics or of military violence, and to judge from the oldest texts, he wasn't a monarchist either — in his sermons the word *rājā* ('king') was often pronounced together with the word *cora* ('thief' — in Thailand today, that would probably have been cause enough to put him in prison for lese-majesty!), he criticized the system of hereditary offices, and besides, he had started his own career by running away from home so he wouldn't have to inherit a throne. In any case he did give some advice, but maybe not of quite that kind that Ajātasattu had expected. He told the king's minister what advice he once had given to Vajji to help them keep its position as a free republic, and he said that as long as Vajji followed this advice — and this they had done so far — trying to invade their country wasn't any use.

The essence of the advice was that the republic's citizens should meet often and discuss their common problems, and that many should come to the meetings; that they should make and execute their decisions in concord; that they shouldn't unnecessarily adopt new laws or abolish old ones, but continue to follow their old republican customs; that they should respect old people and like to listen to them; that they should respect women and not practice rape or abductions; that they should show respect to their country's old shrines; and that they should protect and defend the *arahants* living in their country.

[As to the choice between republic and monarchy, Buddhist tradition would strongly deviate from the Buddha's own opinion after some centuries, when more and more monarchs, and more and more powerful ones, showed an interest in supporting and exploiting Buddhism. From the reasons mentioned above I hope it should be clear, though, that, e.g., the fanatical monarchism of present-day Thailand has absolutely no support in the Buddha's teaching.]

The Buddha then continued his wanderings, together with a great number of friars. His last rainy season he spent near Vesālī/Vaiśalī. When the rains had just begun, he was attacked with violent and deadly pains. As usual he didn't complain. He could have died then and there, but he decided to devote all his will-power to go on living until he had time to take leave of the friars, who at that time were dispersed throughout a great part of India. During these rains, the Buddha also was informed that Sāriputta and Moggallāna had just passed away.

Now Ānanda reminded the Buddha about what religious teachers used to see as their duty: to appoint a successor before they died. But the Buddha refused. What he had to give, he had given openly. He had not had 'the teacher's closed fist' (*acariyamutthi*), and he had not made any difference between an exoteric doctrine and an esoteric one (*anantaram abahiram*). When he was dead, the *Dhamma* should be their teacher, not any specific individual.

[Thus, according to these sources, there can't be any 'esoteric Buddhism'. Later schools claiming to be just that quite simply aren't Buddhist. Tibetan Rinpoches may say that 'the *sūtras* can be considered the exoteric teaching of Buddha and the Tantras his esoteric teaching', but the Buddha himself evidently disagreed — or would have done so if Tantrism had at all existed in his time. Most probably it didn't arise until a thousand years later.

By taking such a position as he did, the Buddha rejected the Indian *guru* system; but in many later Buddhist traditions, it has crept in again. Zen Buddhism, e.g., is counting with a series of patriarchs, beginning with the Buddha himself and his alleged successor Kassapa/Kasyapa, and Tibetan tradition has even added to the three Buddhist refuges—to the Buddha, the *Dhamma* and the *saṁgha* — a fourth one (recited even before the three canonical ones!) to the Lama, i.e., *guru*, who is sometimes said to be necessary for one's own enlightenment. Both cases are clear deviations from what is said in the oldest canonical texts.]

After the rains, the wanderings continued. At the full moon day of February, the Buddha decided to live for three months more, and that would have to be enough.

When the three months had passed, the Buddha and some friars had lunch at the house of a goldsmith (or perhaps blacksmith — the meaning of the Pāli word is discussed among the linguists) named Cuṇḍa. Among the courses served there was one, called in Pāli *sūkara-maddava*, which literally means 'swine-sweets'. What it actually was is not certain. Learned men are still discussing whether it is something sweet from pigs, i.e., pork, or something which pigs find sweet, e. g., truffles.

In any case the Buddha asked that this dish should be served only to him, while the friars would have to content themselves with all the others, and that what was left of the swine-sweets would then be buried in the ground, for there was no one else that could digest it.

It seems that the pork, or truffle, or whatever it was, had gone past its 'To Be Consumed Before'-date; for after this meal, the Buddha once again got some deadly pains. He didn't complain. Instead he, in the company of Ānanda and other friars, went to the village of Kusinārā/Kuśinagara (nowadays a couple of miles from the town of Kasiya, near the bigger town of Gorakhpur in north India, close to the Nepalese border; also not very far from Sāvatthī/Śrāvastī, where he had spent so many rainy seasons, or from Lumbinī, where he was born, now at the Nepalese side of the border). There he lay down between two trees, and there gathered many friars and laymen. The Buddha gave them his last instructions. Then he entered some deep meditative states (which is *not* the same thing as a coma! There are very learned scholars who can't distinguish the two concepts . . .), and then he died very quietly and fully aware.

The death of the Buddha is the starting-point of Buddhist chronology. There are two versions of this: one Western in India, Ceylon, and Burma, with the death year called year 1, and one Eastern in Siam, Laos, and Cambodia, where it is called year 0. Thus there is a difference by 1, although both ways are counting with the same death year (which probably is wrong, just as the calculated birth year of Jesus as starting point of Christian chronology). The Jubilee Year of 2500 (*Buddha Jayanti*) occurred in 1956 according to Western tradition, but in 1957 according to the Eastern one. In 1956, because of this jubilee, was finished the Sixth Buddhist Council according to South Buddhist tradition in Rangoon, Burma.

The alleged founders of the three world religions — Siddhattha Gotama, Jesus, and Mohammed — have almost certainly existed as historical figures; but to Buddhists this matter is, as I have already suggested, much less important than to Christians or Muslims. One reason why I personally believe the Buddha to have actually existed, however, is the fact that the oldest texts describe him in a way which makes him, from a *literary* point of view, not interesting at all. Novels have been written about Jesus, and if not so many have been written about Mohammed, the reasons for that are not literary ones. The lives of both were filled with the kind of conflicts that good stories are made of. The Buddha, on the other hand, is described as perfectly balanced and never letting himself be provoked; and that is not the kind of character that writers use to invent. And sure enough, not many stories have been written about the Buddha, at least not about his time of *being* Buddha, i.e., after awakening. What *has* been written have mostly been about Prince Siddhattha's life *before* becoming Buddha, or else about the people around him rather than about himself. Even this chapter may be an example of this. . .

On the other hand, the Buddha has always caused great interest as a human example, and for painters and sculptors, the Buddha image is one of the greatest challenges. This, I believe, may be the real reason why such images were not created until long after the Buddha's death. (Some authors have believed this to be due to an original prohibition against imagery, but such rules belong to Judaism, Islam, and some branches of Christianity, not to South Asian traditions.)

Certain elements in later Buddha images have, by the way, caused some strange misconceptions. Many Asians believe the Buddha to have been many times as big as a normal man, because some artists have, for symbolical reasons, depicted him as such. The *Tipiṭaka* says nothing of the kind. What it *does* say is that at one time he exchanged his robe with that of the friar Kassapa, and that the robe of the friar Nanda (according to the *Vinaya Piṭaka, Suttavibhaṅga, Pacittīya,* 92) had the same size as the one of the Buddha, which would have been unlikely indeed if one of them had been several times as tall as the other.

In the West it is a common idea that the Buddha was, if not a giant, then at least clearly overweight — 'as fat as a Buddha'. The *Tipiṭaka* doesn't say anything about this either, nor is he depicted that way in Buddhist art; but there are Chinese pictures of a *Bodhisattva*, i.e., as someone who will *become* a Buddha — not Gotama, or anyone else who already is one — with an imposing paunch, and some Westerners don't care to check up what is what.

Christian people often speak about their god as 'Our

Father'; but if a good father is expected to help his children to grow to his own level, that isn't quite proper, for according to Christianity (and Islam) a man can never become a god. The word 'father' actually suits the Buddha better, for according to him, Buddhahood is open for everyone who makes the necessary effort and sacrifice.

The character of the Buddha Gotama has caused a great interest also in non-Buddhist circles, which has often been a good reason for mixed feelings among Buddhists. Hinduism has in-defined the Buddha as the ninth *avatāra* (incarnation) of its god Viṣṇu. [Actually, what we call Hinduism today is so different from Brāhmaṇism at the time of the Buddha — not least because of influence from Buddhism, but also from Islam, which even brought to India the Persian (!) word 'Hindu' — that Hinduism should be regarded as a younger religion than Buddhism.] Some Muslims are regarding the Buddha as one of God's prophets, although he expressly rejected such monotheistic reasonings as did exist in certain schools of thought at his time, and although he quite as expressly advised us not to trust revelations. There are also Christians who like to see the Buddha as a predecessor of Christ's, which can be refuted by the same reasons. [It is a different question how far certain parts of the doctrine of Jesus and the oldest Christian church, and especially their ethics, may have been influenced by Buddhism.]

The story about the Buddha-to-be and his life went further west than his teaching. In the Muslim world, the word *Bodhisattva* was distorted into *Budasp*. In the Caucasus this became *Joasaf*, and in Latin *Josafat*. Details were 'bettered' a lot during the process, and in medieval times, the story had turned into a Christian legend. (It may be found in several collections, e.g., in Latin in the *Legenda Aurea*.) Saint Josafat, prince of India, was an official saint of the Catholic church for very long, until they finally found out who he was. The Orthodox churches, e.g., those of Greece and Russia, also included him in their calenders, and unlike the Catholic one they don't have any centralized and formal way of judicially deciding who shall be canonized, and perhaps de-canonized, so he is said still to be there.

Later Western religions or pseudo-religions, from Theosophy to New Age, have often included some chosen parts of Buddhism torn out of context, and not rarely confused with Hindu ideas (in the pretty but completely groundless thought that all religions really teach the same thing). It is a disquieting tendency, when certain groups or individuals are practising Buddhist meditation without caring about Buddhist morality and the Buddhist view of society. The Buddha's teaching is no toy for ego-trippers, and meditation without morality is dangerous.

Therefore, it is important to try to get an overall picture of whom the Buddha actually meant himself to be, and what he actually wanted to say.

2

The Teaching (Dhamma)

SOMETHING characteristic for Buddhism, and distinguishing it from most other religions, is its empirical foundation. A Buddhist starts from what he knows, and from there he is searching his way to that which he knows not. He doesn't claim to know all, but neither does he build his life on that which he doesn't know. Christians and Muslims are demanded by their faiths to do just that, and many others do it too, but according to Buddhism, that is equivalent to building one's house upon the sand.

Buddhism is strictly atheistic. (Some English-speakers prefer to call it 'non-theistic', because they think the word 'atheist' is pejorative, which it isn't. An atheist is quite simply someone who doesn't believe in God, and the Buddha didn't do that, and neither do his followers, if they *are* his followers; so we Buddhists *should* be atheists, and make no fuss about it.) On the other hand, Buddhism is *not* materialistic. From that fact, Marxists and other dualists have come to the conclusion that Buddhism is idealistic; but original Buddhism isn't that either (although some later traditions have evolved in that direction).

To give a rough definition, materialism says that matter was first, and that mind arose later. So think most Western atheists, and it is also the working hypothesis of secular science (though many astronomers are speaking sloppishly about 'creation' when a Buddhist would say 'arising', which mostly is what the astronomers actually mean). Idealism, on the other hand, says that some kind of mind (e. g., the thought of God or some kind of World Spirit) comes before all matter; that mind comes first, and that matter is created by or arises from mind.

These two views have one thing in common: they both presuppose a first beginning. Buddhism doesn't accept that premise. It isn't at all taken for granted in the philosophical tradition of India, while Greeks and Westerners have often seen it as self-evident.

Thus, Buddhism is neither materalistic nor idealistic. The basic opinion of Buddhism is that both views are right, and that both are wrong. Mind presupposes matter, *and* matter presupposes mind, in a beginningless interaction. If the universe we know has a first beginning, whether Big-Bang or something else, then it can't be '*the* universe', i.e., everything that is, for *e nihilo nihil*, from nothing comes nothing. (Really, the word 'universe' should only be used about what some physicists today call the 'multiverse', i.e., the sum total of our 'universe' and all others.) Our cosmos can't exist without a cause. So far Buddhists agree with Creationists; but unlike these, Buddhism adds that such a cause, e.g. a possible creator, also couldn't exist without having a cause of its own. Thus, the chain of cause and effect just can't have a first beginning.

From this also follows that searching for an ultimate meaning of life is meaningless; for if you should find a meaning of life, you could always go on to ask about the meaning of the meaning, and the meaning of the meaning of the meaning, and so on *ad infinitum.* Buddhism recommends us to live here and now, and to *give* a meaning to life, not to lose ourselves in speculations about that which we don't know.

Thus, Buddhism doesn't accept the idea of an omnipotent creator god. There are also other logical reasons not to accept the concept of omnipotence, such as the question "If God is omnipotent, can he then, *without going beyond the rules of human logic,* create a stone that is so heavy that even he can't lift it?" However that question is answered, omnipotence is refuted.

Another reason is an ethical one. Christianity and Islam teach that God has all power but no responsibility, while man has all responsibility and (by logical necessity, though it may not be said explicitly) no power. Buddhism does not accept such a separation of power and responsibility. If one being had all the power there is, he would by necessity also have all the guilt there is. It is logically impossible for an omnipotent being to be good. Therefore, every worship of an omnipotence is really a kind of devil-worship. Praying to an almighty being means kneeling down to evil, consciously or unconsciously.

Many god-believers have — after a couple of millennia of trying, as diligently as fruitlessly, to explain how one and the same god could be both almighty, all-knowing and all good *and* permit evil to exist — retired to the position that reason must halt at this question. Buddhism does not accept such an intellectual capitulation. Buddhism is *trans*-intellectual, but (in its original form) not *anti*-intellectual (though many later 'masters' are). It doesn't claim that intellectual reason can understand everything — liberating insight belongs to a plane beyond the intellectual one — but neither does it accept the assertion that what logic clearly shows to be impossible may still be true, still less that anyone is eternally damned for refusing to believe in that which just isn't true (e.g. the possibility of a good omnipotence).

The world, Buddhism says, is not ruled according to some divine plan; but that doesn't mean that it is ruled by chance. Buddhism speaks about cause and effect, by 'natural laws' that are not laws in the juridical sense of the word — no one made them — and that also are not quite identical with those generalized experiences which we ordinarily call 'natural laws', as science doesn't know everything.

And probably never will, since reality is more complex than mankind's collected thought-power. And the Buddha never taught everything there is. He didn't even teach everything he knew, just a little of it; and he said that what he did teach was a much in comparison to what he knew, as those leaves he could take in his hand were to all leaves growing in the Indian rain-forest.

What he did teach was the Four Noble Truths about unsatisfactoriness, the cause of unsatisfactoriness, the end of unsatisfactoriness, and the way to the end of unsatisfactoriness. (This formulation may be somewhat clumsy in English, but I think it will have to do. The common translations of 'suffering' or 'pain' just don't cover the meaning of the fundamental concept of *dukkha/duḥkha,* and would have to be accompanied by some kind of foot-note or other explanation, which would be even clumsier.)

The Four Noble Truths are the most fundamental part of Buddhism, so fundamental that they were the first thing the Buddha taught to the five Samaṇas. But they are also so advanced that he, when teaching people less mentally developed than they, never used to explain them without having prepared the listener by speaking about elementary morality (which would turn up again in the Fourth Noble Truth).

The First Noble Truth does *not* say that 'everything is suffering', as has often been claimed by early writers who didn't know better, and unfortunately also by some later ones who should do it. [And I suspect that some of them do. In my own country, this gross misrepresentation has even crept into our very recent National Encyclopaedia, in the article

'Buddhism' written by Prof. Peter Schalk of Upsala: one of the many who, when the Berlin Wall fell, suddenly stopped having ever been a Marxist, and generally regarded — by my countrymen, but not by me — as Sweden's foremost living authority on Buddhism, and as one of the foremost on Sri Lankan and Indian affairs. He doesn't understand non-dualist thinking, but he *has* studied Pāli.]

The English phrase 'everything is suffering' is a mistranslation of the Pāli phrase *sabbe saṇkhārā dukkhā,* which I think may best be translated by 'all conditioned things are unsatisfactory'. In the mistranslation, there are two serious mistakes. Firstly, *dukkha* is a concept which does include that which is in English calles 'suffering', but also much more. *Dukkha* is everything that won't give you a *permanent* satisfaction. Suffering and pain don't do it, but neither do impermanent pleasure and happiness, if we cling to them when they cease; which we will do, more or less, as long as we are not *arahants*.

Secondly, the erroneous translation has excluded the word *saṅkhāra/saṁskāra,* 'conditioned' or 'compounded'. Well, Buddhism does teach that everything is conditioned except *nibbāna,* but that little exception is very important indeed, as it is the precondition of the third and fourth Noble Truths — the end of unsatisfactoriness, and the way.

The phrase 'all conditioned things are unsatisfactory' is one of three phrases, in Pāli *sabbe saṅkhārā aniccā, sabbe saṅkhārā dukkhā, sabbe dhammā anattā*: "all conditioned things are impermanent, all conditioned things are unsatisfactory, all things are not me". In the third phrase the word *saṅkhāra* has been replaced by *dhamma,* which has several meanings, but here it may be translated quite simply by 'thing' or 'phenomenon'. The difference between *sabbe saṅkhārā* and *sabbe dhammā* is the fact that the first includes everything *except nibbāna,* while the second comprises everything *including nibbāna.* This third phrase is aimed at one of man's most treasured self-delusions, and a central dogma in many religions: the thought that man has some kind of eternal core, an immortal soul or spirit, which doesn't really change, but is either reincarnated (as in Hinduism) or destined to experience, after the death of the body, either eternal bliss or eternal damnation (as in *post-biblical* Christianity, which is strongly influenced by Old Greek idealism. *Biblical* Christianity, interestingly enough, doesn't say a word about an immortal soul. Instead, it teaches the resurrection of the body, which is something quite different). Thus rebirth, as seen by Buddhism, is *not* reincarnation. There is no eternal soul entering a series of temporal bodies, but a physical and mental process, the different stages of which are joined together by a *continuity* but not *identity*.

In his first sermon, the Buddha formulated the First Noble Truth thus:

> Birth is unsatisfactory, ageing is unsatisfactory, illness is unsatisfactory, death is unsatisfactory, presence of what is not dear is unsatisfactory, absence of what is dear is unsatisfactory, the unfulfilled wish — that too is unsatisfactory. In short: the five aggregates of clinging are unsatisfactory.

By 'the five aggregates of clinging' (*pañc-ûpādāna-khandhā*) is meant the five components of a living being, and especially a human one: body, feelings, perceptions, wishes and consciousnesses.

Please note consciousness*es*, in plural! A consciousness is, according to Buddhist psychology, nothing which lasts for very long. It is an extremely fleeting phenomenon, arising when there is contact between a sense-organ and a sense-object. If we see 'our consciousness' as a self or me, as many do (even some psychologists), this is because we have not observed and analyzed it sufficiently.

Neither should one, as many people also do, confuse consciousness with mind as a whole. When Buddhism is talking of the five components of man, four of these are mental, but consciousnesses are only one of these four elements. A feeling, perception or wish is not conscious in itself, but there may — sometimes, but not every time — arise a consciousness *about* that feeling, perception, or wish. We must not imagine that we wish only what we *know* that we wish. Desire does not presuppose consciousness.

The second Noble Truth, about the cause of unsatisfactoriness, is running thus in the same text:

> It is just this thirst leading to rebirth, connected with pleasure and passion, delighting now in this, now in that, namely thirst for sense-pleasure, thirst for becoming, thirst for annihilation.

In earlier Western versions, the last concept was often mistranslated by 'thirst for richness' or something similar. The Pāli word *vibhava* is, annoyingly enough, a homonym with two widely different meanings: 'richness' and 'annihilation'. But when the classical commentaries became available, it turned out that what the Buddha was speaking of really was death urge, on a level with life urge — two-and-a-half millennia before Freud! It is important, thus, not to confuse freedom from desire with desire for expiry.

The third Noble Truth, about the end of unsatisfactoriness, is running thus:

> It is the completely passionless ceasing of just this thirst, the giving up of it, the renunciation of it, the liberation from it, the distaste of it.

The word 'distaste' should here be taken in its literal sense — just a dis-taste — without any violently emotional rejecting being involved.

The fourth Noble Truth, about the method to end unsatisfactoriness, says that this is

> just this Noble Eightfold Path, namely right view, right thought, right speech, right action, right profession, right effort, right attention, right concentration.

These eight points summarize all of the Buddhist way of life. They should not be understood as stages — it is not possible to develop, e.g., right view without training the other parts of the way as well. With a modern metaphor one could perhaps call it 'a road of eight traffic lanes'. An older simile is a rope of eight parts. If you want to use that rope for climbing, you must grip them all.

The eight points may be divided into two main sections: morality and meditation; or into three, if meditation is in its turn divided into concentration training and insight training. This distinction is very important in Buddhist contexts, since moral and concentration training may be found in many religions, while only Buddhism offers insight training.

Quite properly, insight training (*vipassanā/vipaśyanā*) is mentioned first. Right view and right thought belong to it. Their position at the head of the list means that a certain degree of right understanding of reality, and of right thinking, is necessary already as a precondition of good morality and concentration; but insight can't, according to Buddhism, be perfected without development of morality and concentration. The goal of insight training is liberating wisdom or insight (*paññā/prajñā*).

Moral or ethical training comprises the three next points: right speech, right action and right profession. The fact that right profession or livelihood is mentioned separately, instead of just being included in right action, shows that the Buddha was not indifferent to economical matters. The three points mean, in short, that one should train oneself to talk and act as litte as possible in ways that hurt oneself or others, and as much as possible in ways that help oneself and others.

It is important to point out that in Buddhism, morality too is a matter of *training*, and that all training is gradual. Buddhism is fundamentally anti-fundamentalist. It doesn't make the common mistake of some other religions first to demand that man be perfect and then, when he doesn't manage to be that just at once without even having got some tips about how to train, ascribe to him some kind of original sin and declare that he is depraved by nature. Buddhism believes neither in original sin nor (in its original form) in salvation by grace. We are not perfect, but whatever happens to be our present level, we can always take another step forward, and another, and another. . .

[There are later traditions that seem to deviate strongly from this original rejection of the idea of grace, e.g., Japanese Shin Buddhism; but not even there the difference in comparison to original Buddhism, or the similarity to Christianity, was as big to begin with as might be believed at first sight. The Buddha Amitābha, who is invoked in Shin Buddhism, is *not* seen as an omnipotent creator of our world. He is said, just as any Buddha, to have begun his career as an ordinary man. Besides, it may be true that he, according to this tradition, is said to be able to help his faithful ones to be reborn in his country; but that country is not really seen as something *instead* of *nibbāna,* but as an environment with the best conditions possible to attain *nibbāna* by ones own striving.]

Perhaps it was just because of this gradual training that the Buddha refused to decree any kind of special diet even to the friars, still less to the laity. Some later traditions have asserted that every real Buddhist must be a vegetarian, and there are even 'Buddhist' sects who don't permit their members to eat onions or garlic; but such rules are not supported in the least by the oldest sources. According to them, demands for a compulsory vegetarianism were brought up by Devadatta the Traitor, and expressly rejected by the Buddha.

This may also be a consolation to those who are trying to find a 'right profession' in a capitalistic labour-market. After all, market economy does hardly support a higher morality. Buddhism doesn't condemn those who, out of economical necessity, end up in a morally doubtful profession.

If, on the other hand, e.g., hunting or fishing is practised *for pleasure* and not for survival, then it isn't a matter of livelihood any more but of action. In such a case, Buddhism is clearly negative.

According to Ceylonese tradition, Buddhism was brought to the island by a friar, who first of all made the local king stop hunting. In my own country, the present king of Sweden is *very* fond of hunting and fishing, so according to Buddhist norms, he is in this respect a bad example. We do have some Theravāda friars here, both Sinhalese and Thai, but they haven't been able to talk him out of it. (If I am to be perfectly honest, I don't thing they've tried.)

Buddhism doesn't like any kind of intentional killing, whether the victims are human or animal. In this matter however, same as in others, it does admit a difference in degree between different kinds of wrong action. Buddhism judges the moral quality of an action mainly from the intentions behind it, rather than from its results — your intentions are within yourself, so you can gradually learn to control them, but you will never be able to control all the practical effects of your actions — so killing is also held to be worse the more energy and decisiveness you exercise when you kill.

As a result of this attitude Buddhism, unlike Christianity, has not only replaced bloody sacrifice of animals with the bloodless sacrifice of 'holy' mass, but quite rejected the very thought of bloody sacrifice as fundamentally unhealthy. Many Buddhists are nauseated by Christian 'Holy Supper' and Jewish Torah recitation, if they know what the Christians are supposed to sup and what the Jewish cantor is actually reading, since both rites do mean that their practisers are regarding ritual killing as something meritorious. Unlike Jesus, the Buddha would never have felt at home in a temple which was in fact a slaughter-house.

The resolution not to kill is the first of five training-rules, which are the foundation of Buddhist morality, and which every active Buddhist is in principle expected to esteem. It must be said, however, that these training-rules are just that, and no commandments. They are formulated in first person (as Western grammars number them; Indian grammars call it the third): '*I* accept the training-rule to. . .', and not in second person with any '*Thou* shalt'.

These five training-rules are for exercising the abstention from

1. damaging life,
2. taking that which isn't given,
3. wrong conduct in sense-pleasures,
4. false speech,
5. intoxication.

The second rule means not taking that which one knows is someone else's, unless that one has given it away.

The third rule was interpreted already by the classical commentarians as 'wrong conduct in sex', according to the principle widely practised in religious circles: "I Dislike All Kinds of Immorality, But I Dislike *Sexual* Immorality With a

Special Interest." But 'sense pleasure' (*kāma*) is a wider concept. For friars (and for those laypeople who so wish), this rule is exchanged for a stricter one demanding celibacy. Others are told by the rule not to satisfy their desires in ways damaging to themselves, to partners if any, or to third parties. Later commentators have specified this rule and invented lists of specific actions, especially sexual ones, but to the Buddha himself, the important thing was rather the spirit of the action. A loving man won't rape, but not all non-raping men are loving, so it isn't an indifferent matter in which end to begin.

The fourth rule is the central one of 'right speech', but it does also include 'right thought', for its fundamental meaning is honesty to oneself, and thereby to others. On the other hand, it does *not* mean that everything that's true must necessarily be said. Buddhism does not encourage gossip, however true it may be (and whatever number of 'Buddhists' may love it). The Buddhist ideal is honesty combined with consideration and loving-kindness.

Lies should not be said, but even truths should be said only if useful. Whether they are pleasant or not to those concerned is not important, though. Unpalatable truths may, if told at the right moment, do more good than flattery.

The fifth rule doesn't care *how* you intoxicate yourself. Its great importance is the Buddhist combination of morality and meditation. Mindfulness is difficult enough as it is, and drugs or liquor won't make it easier.

Actually, right action and right speech will always touch right thought. The five rules are negatively formulated, but when psychologically extended, they will also have a positive aspect. Not to kill is the first step in the cultivation of Buddhist love (*mettā/maitrī*, which—unlike the closest Christian concept, called in Greek *agapē* and in Latin *caritas*— is to be extended to *all* living beings, not only human and divine ones, but also animals; *and* devils, if any should happen to exist). Not to take what isn't given is the first step in the cultivation of generosity.

Parts of concentration training, finally, are the three last points of the way (last in the list, but not in the training): right effort, right attention, right concentration. These three together comprise what most non-Buddhists call 'meditation', but which for Buddhists is just a foundation for the really deciding kind of meditation: insight training; and so we are back again at the two first points of the way. Full concentration — *samādhi* — is, for Buddhism (unlike Hinduism and Theosophy), *not* the highest goal, but at best a helpful support when trying to achieve it, at worst a trap. One may get so attached to inner peace that one completely forgets liberation.

Already in the oldest sources, the Buddhist way is called the 'Middle Path' (in Pāli *majjhima paṭipadā*). That phrase should not be misunderstood. The middle way of Buddhism does not lead to a middling goal, and it is not an expression of some kind of centre politics. It is a way between two ditches, which are preferably not to be fallen into by those who wish to walk the path unto its end: hedonism and flagellantism. It is a middle path leading to the most extreme goal possible: complete freedom from greed, hatred, and delusion.

Buddhism is no faith, and its teaching is a map — not a collection of dogmas. Man's task, according to Buddhism, is not to glorify an unknown god who, for some reason, seems to address the individual only through some rather faulty middlemen, who have never been able to prove even that their alleged principal exists; but to be as great a blessing as possible both to oneself and to others by freeing oneself, gradually, from greed, hatred, and delusion.

Buddhism is a map, and every map is a simplification. The Buddha did not reproduce all the details of the terrain. Instead, he gave us a tool to find our way in it for ourselves. In Buddhist tradition, as in other traditions, not all have understood this, and some commentators have shown greater interest in the separate words of the Buddha's sermons than in trying to figure what he actually was trying to say, and how that could be applied in another time and place.

Buddhism is not so extremely relativistic as to deny the existence of absolute truth, but it does maintain that absolute truth can be understood only by someone absolutely free from greed, hatred, and delusion. Everything the rest of us can perceive — whether we are human, divine, or something else, and however powerful we happen to be — is, at best, relative truths.

Divine revelations are, as Buddhism sees it, no reliable source of information, for several reasons. Firstly, it is very difficult to distinguish actual revelations of possible beings in other dimensions from projections out of one's own subconscious. Secondly, it would, if we did get a revelation, not be easy for us to know whether the being revealing himself is honest to us or a liar. Thirdly, we would, even if that being were honest, not easily be able to know whether said being were actually knowing what he were talking about, *especially* if his knowledge and power were vastly superior to ours. The more superior to us someone is, the greater is the chance that we overestimate him. The fact that someone is knowing enormously much more than we do doesn't necessarily mean, after all, that he knows everything; and as to power, it is never combined with real wisdom, so if a god were omnipotent (if that were at all possible, which for logical reasons it isn't, as has been already pointed out), he would, *because of his omnipotence*, be a complete idiot. A god is, according to Buddhism, no authority.

In the *Dīgha Nikāya* of the *Tipiṭaka*, there is a story of a *deva* dying in a high 'heaven' and being born in a somewhat lower one, where he happens to come first. He is feeling lonely and wishes to have some other beings around. At the same moment, some others die in the higher heaven and are reborn near him. Then he imagines himself to have created them, and they too share his illusion; but what had actually happened was that he happened to be the first-comer in a specific world, not in all worlds.

This story is a critique of the thought of an omnipotent god, which did exist in India at the time of the Buddha, but which wasn't universally prevailing. In later centuries, the vast propagation of Christianity and Islam has sometimes made it extremely dangerous to criticize that idea (as it had also been in Old Testament Judaism, though that was at least in more limited circles); but according to Buddhism, such a criticism is perfectly legitimate.

It should be pointed out, in this context, that Buddhist moral rules really concern morality. They are not mixed up with allegedly divine, but ethically irrelevant, decrees to have 'no other gods before me'. That rule has never been accepted by Buddhism.

This story, about a very powerful but rather stupid 'god' being reborn and believing himself to be the creator of all things visible and invisible, brings us to the Buddhist view of the next life, which is connected to the Buddhist view of *this* life, which is connected to Buddhist psychology. Many Western scholars believe that psychology is a fairly new science, and they devote much effort to reinventing the wheel, because they've got the idea that the intellectual world has its eastern limits at the Bosphorus. Many are also trying to talk about the Buddhist thought of rebirth without knowing its psychological background, confusing rebirth and reincarnation, which are two completely different things. [There are even some who then confuse this mixture, muddled enough in itself, with the belief of some Christian thinkers, e.g., Origene, in the preexistence of the soul, which has nothing to do with the other two; thus bringing intellectual disorder to its completion.]

The basic idea of the Buddhist rebirth theory is the thought that a possible next life — the belief in which is not compulsory for Buddhists, as Buddhism isn't a belief — must be subject to the same basic conditions as this life. It must be time-bound, and therefore impermanent, and therefore unsatisfactory.

Buddhism does not accept the thought of life eternal. Among those religions and individuals that do believe in it, there are two quite different opinions about what 'life eternal' actually means. Some regard eternity as infinite time, others as timelessness. Life eternal according to the latter alternative is refuted by the fact that all life is change, and change can only take place in time. All perception, too, presupposes movement, and movement is not possible without time. Thus, a timeless state would by logical necessity be a state without movement and change, without vibrations and therefore without perceptions. Actually, it wouldn't be a state at all. Actually, it wouldn't be at all.

If, on the other hand, there were a life infinitely extended in time, the accumulated changes would finally be so great that there wouldn't be an identity any more, in spite of continuity. Thus, there wouldn't be one and the same being living infinitely.

And the same thing is true already about this life itself. A new-born baby is not identical with the ten-year-old child who will one decade later have the same name and social security number, the ten-year-old is not identical with the twenty-year-old still ten years later, and so on. The one who is dying is not identical with the one who was born, and the one who is possibly reborn cannot, by the same reason, be identical with the one who died. It is not a matter of identity but of continuity. There is no permanent self.

What is keeping this continuity together is, according to Buddhism, that which is called in Pāli *kamma* and in Sanskrit *karma.* The Sanskrit form of this word is used also outside Buddhism, and it may then have several quite different meanings. In Buddhism, *kamma/karma* means that volition which is behind every intentional action, and which will give its mental stamp to the actor, more or less deeply. Thus *kamma* is, according to Buddhism, not the action itself but the intention behind it (unintentional actions don't make *kamma*). Neither does the word *kamma* cover the two concepts of cause and effect, as can sometimes be read; just the cause. The effect of this cause is called *vipāka.*

The creator of *kamma* is not identical with the reaper of *vipāka,* even if *kamma* and *vipāka* occur within the same physical life. Neither is the creator of *kamma* someone else than the reaper of *vipāka,* even if *kamma* and *vipāka* occur in different physical lives. No identity is there, but for certain a continuity, both within the single physical life and in all the chain of lives kammically knit together.

As usual, it should be emphasized that the Buddhist doctrine of *kamma* and *vipāka* isn't a dogma to believe in, but a formulation of experiences done by earlier Buddhists; a map to help you find your way in the terrain. Testing it by compairing it with the terrain is perfectly allowed.

It should also be pointed out that *kamma,* according to Buddhism, is one factor affecting life, but not the only one. Buddhism does not deny influence from external causes such as climate, inheritance and environment. There is also a basic principle in Buddhist philosophy that *each cause has more than one effect, and each effect has more than one cause.* Thus, Buddhism does not search a single cause of everything that is, and causal connections are seen as a net rather than a chain. Since man is a social being, the *kamma* of different individuals will also affect each other.

Different forms of *karma*-concepts can be found in many different thought-systems. There are non-Buddhist teachings where *karma* is seen from the point of view of the onlooker, and where it may be taken as an excuse not to engage oneself socially, to say that the poor and unhappy people should blame themselves when reaping the fruits of earlier *karma.*

According to Buddhism, such a callous attitude itself will make bad *kamma.* At the sight of a suffering fellow being one should, says Buddhism, not primarily ask oneself what this being might have done to deserve his suffering; those causal connections are so complex and hidden that not even all *arahants* are able to discern them, and *kamma* is, as has already been pointed out, not the only cause of suffering. What's important is how to act oneself towards those who suffer. Sincere compassion and active help (as to capacity) will make good *kamma* to the actor; coldheartedness and passivity in front of suffering will make bad *kamma.* Buddhism is, first and last, own action.

In such a perspective, there will be no conflict between egoism and altruism. Who doesn't care about his own good will in the long run not be able to help others (if I love my neighbour as myself without loving myself, that will be of little use to my neighbour; and 'the Golden Rule', in its 'positive' version, should preferably not be practised by masochists), and who doesn't care about the good of others are not likely to get rid of that self-illusion, which Buddhism helds to be the ultimate cause of our mental captivity.

Many Westerners think that Buddhism is some kind of individualism. Most Asian Buddhists don't understand this, since individualism is a typically Western phenomenon, and historically speaking not a very old one.

Admittedly, Buddhism does emphasize individual man's responsibility, and it doesn't accept any demands for blind obedience, whether it be towards the family head, an alleged deity, or the laws of the country — neither law nor tradition must ever be placed above morality. Buddhism is not as extremely collectivistic as mainstream Christianity and mainstream Islam. It has nothing corresponding to the Sunday duty of Christianity or the Friday duty of Islam, and it does not admit (as does, e.g., Catholicism) that an ecclesiastical authority may under certain circumstances be given greater weight than your own conscience. [It is careful, though, to make a distinction between conscience and selfish desire.] Buddhism has never had any pope or caliph. [No, the Dalai Lama isn't one. He is the leader of a national tradition within Buddhism, and partly without it, and mass media have made him the most famous individual Buddhist of our times; but he is not the leader of all Buddhists, and he has never shown any signs of wanting to.]

But if Buddhism doesn't prescribe any ritual duties, it does attach a very great importance to active love and active compassion. Buddhist life is morality and meditation, and morality comes first. Thus, Buddhism is *not* a way to individual liberation *only*. Such a liberation is, according to Buddhism, not possible without a social engagement.

On the other hand, a good society can't be built by bad people. Meditation is no substitute for practical work, but practical work can very easily go wrong if it isn't built on some kind of meditation. If you wish to have a go at developing society, you must first of all develop yourself.

Buddhism doesn't give any ready-made solutions to the problems of specific societies, as the Buddha was fully aware that societies change. Buddhism gives some fundamental moral principles, which it would be wise for all to follow: not to kill or hurt intentionally, not to steal intentionally, not to seek pleasures in ways damaging to oneself or to others, not to lie, not to intoxicate oneself. If you are unlucky enough to have power over others — which, according to Buddhism, isn't desirable at all — there is of list of ten duties of a ruler: generosity, morality, sacrifice, honesty, kindness, simple habits, freedom from anger, non-violence, patience, and freedom from obstruction of the people's will.

I don't think it's very easy to find in history a single ruler who has lived up to these ten rules. I also don't think it's very easy to find someone who *did* more or less live up to them, who didn't do everything he could *not* to get power over others. It is clear, from several places in the oldest texts, that the best thing a ruler can do, according to Buddhism, is to abdicate. It is also clear, from the already mentioned advice to Ajātasattu when he planned to invade a neighbouring republic, that the Buddha preferred a common decision-making to autocracy, and that he probably preferred a republican society to a monarchistic one.

Original Buddhism is very critital to all kinds of hierarchies. In a hierarchy, whether secular or 'holy' (which in Greek is *hieros*), the wisest members almost never end up at the top. All power corrupts, and all-power all-corrupts. Buddhism teaches as to bow deep to wisdom and insight, but to keep our backs very straight indeed in front of power, whether it chooses to call itself human or divine.

In Asia, the Buddhist attitude in this matter has not been able to assert itself against age-old cultural traditions. In Thailand, a fanatical monarchism is combined with a state religion called Buddhistic. History can teach us that any kind of state religion will inevitably corrupt both state and religion. So it has been with Christianity in Scandinavia or Britain, so it has been with Islam in Saudi Arabia, Pakistan or Iran, with Hinduism in Nepal, with Judaism in Israel — and with Buddhism in Thailand. Not much is left of the respective religion's original teachings.

The critical spirit of original Buddhism has largely been lost in Asian tradition. In the West, on the other hand, an intellectual climate somewhat similar to the one in India at the time of the Buddha has developed from the Renaissance days and onwards. Today, Buddhism is therefore no less at home in Europe than it is in Asia.

Buddhism has a very pragmatic attitude to rites and ceremonies. You may use them if you need them. If not, don't. The practical result of this has been a lot of different external forms. Each people has formed its own set of ceremonies. An uninformed observer may believe this variation to be an expression of schisms, but a centralized and unified church has never been a Buddhist ideal. In the history of the Christian church, variation is often seen as a result of schisms. In the history of Buddhism, variation is just variation.

The Buddhist view of the importance of fellowship and community is expressed, e.g., in the *Dhammapada*, the stanzas 328-30:

If you get a prudent companion
who is fit to live with you,
who behaves well, and is wise,
you should live with him joyfully and mindfully,
overcoming all dangers.
If you do not get a prudent companion
who is fit to live with you,
who behaves well, and is wise,
then like a king who leaves a conquered kingdom,
you should live alone
as an elephant in the elephant forest.

Better it is to live alone.
There is no fellowship with a fool.
You should live alone doing no evil, and care-free,

like an elephant in the elephant forest.

(Nārada's translation)

Whether you should strive alone or in a group is thus dependent on what groups are available. A good fellowship can be a very good support, but a bad one may be more of a hindrance than a help. Buddhism emphasizes the importance of choosing one's company.

The Pāli and Sanskrit word for 'fellowship' or 'community', is *saṁgha,* and this brings us to the next chapter.

3

The Taught (Saṁgha)

AFTER the death of the Buddha, the history of Buddhism has been carried on by the Buddhist community, the *saṁgha.*

The word *saṁgha* just means 'community' or 'fellowship'. In Buddhist contexts, it has especially three specified meanings:

1. *Bhikkhu-bhikkhunī-saṁgha/bhikṣu-bhikṣuṇī saṁgha*: The community of Buddhist friars and friaresses.
2. *Ariyasaṁgha/āryasaṁgha*: The community of those who have advanced far enough to be either awakened already, or at least certain of becoming so, i.e., those who have become at least *sotapannas*. When a Buddhist takes his refuge in the Buddha, the *Dhamma*, and the *Saṁgha*, this one is primarily meant.
3. The *saṁgha* in the widest sense of the word: the community of all those who are walking the Buddhist path.

Sporadically, other meanings may also be found in the *Tipiṭaka*, e.g., *ñāti-saṁgha*, 'circle of relatives'. In modern Indian languages, the word has got still more meanings: the Soviet Union was in Hindi *Soviyat Saṁgh.*

At first, the Buddhist community grew around the Buddha himself, as was customary in that environment, but he was not only a teacher but also an organizer. He gave to the community a structure able to survive him. As he was working within the framework of Indian Samaṇism, the friars were given a special role in the keeping and teaching of the *Dhamma.* Economical responsibility, on the other hand, was entirely vested with the laity. The friars were not permitted to be gainfully employed or to own money, nor any assets in kind above what was needed for immediate survival.

When the community of friars began to grow, during the life-time of the Buddha, he elaborated am ever more detailed set of rules for the behaviour of the friars, in order to facilitate both the friars' own training in morality and meditation, and the contacts between them and the society around them. For the laity, he recommended a few simple moral training rules — but what is simple isn't necessarily easy.

The Buddha himself was conscious of the fact that many of his rules were motivated by temporary circumstances. Before he died, he gave to the friars his permission to revise them. Those friars who participated in the First Council after his death didn't do that, though, whether due to an exaggerated respect in the Buddha's person (which he himself had advised against) or to a lacking consciousness of how societies change. (According to the *Tipiṭaka,* the reason was that Ānanda had forgot to ask the Buddha exactly what rules he was talking about.) The debate about this started only some centuries later, and as a result the community of friars was then divided into strict and less strict branches. This is the historical basis of the different schools of Buddhism. Philosophical differences, if any, were only formulated later.

The history of Buddhism may be roughly divided into three parts: Buddhism in India from the Buddha to Asoka, Buddhism in Asia from Asoka to Olcott, and Buddhism in the world from Olcott to today.

Buddhism in India: From the Buddha to Asoka

The first important thing to happen after the death and cremation of the Buddha was (according to the *Vinaya Piṭaka, Cullavagga, Khandhaka* 11) that Kassapa/Kaśyapa, who at that time was one of the most respected friars, took an initiative to preserve Buddhism for posterity. The *Saṁgha* was fairly losely organized, and the Buddha hadn't appointed any personal successor, but he had said that henceforward, the *Dhamma* itself should be the teacher of the Buddhists; so the *Dhamma* had to be taken care of.

Although the art of writing was actually invented already at the time, it was used mainly for secular purposes, especially book-keeping. Both paper and printing belonged to the far future, and writing materials were scarce. In India, it was customary that texts meant to be preserved unchanged for a long time were learnt by heart.

To this purpose, Kassapa convened 500 (i.e., many) friars to a First Council in Rājagaha/Rājagṛha during the first rainy season after the Buddha's death. Two friars there were, who remembered most of the Buddha's oral teaching: Upāli regarding the friars' and friaresses' training rules (*vinaya*), and Ānanda regarding the sermons of the Buddha's, and to a certain extent of his foremost disciples (*sutta/sūtra*).

The council began with Kassapa demanding Upāli about the history of the disciplinary rules. Then he demanded Ānanda in the same way about the different sermons: when and where they were given, to whom, about what.

Finally, the council decided what to do about the Buddha's words to Ānanda that the friars, after his death, could modify certain disciplinary rules. Unfortunately, Ānanda had not remembered to ask exactly what rules were meant, and the members of the council didn't dare to decide for themselves, so nothing was changed.

Last of all, there was a dialogue between some conservative friars and Ānanda, illustrating the kind of transit period in which Buddhism was founded. These friars blamed Ānanda for five things: for not having asked the Buddha exactly what rules could be changed; for having, at one occasion, accidentally stepped on the Buddha's robe while sewing it; for having, after the Buddha's death, let women salute the remainders before the men; for neglecting, at one occasion when the Buddha had said that he could live to the end of this age if he was asked to, to ask him to do so; and for having arranged the foundation of an order of friaresses.

Ānanda accepted to call this a fault, out of respect for the other friars, but nevertheless he declared that he didn't see it as one. As to the rules, he hadn't been mindful enough; as to stepping on the robe, it wasn't due to lack of respect; as to letting women salute the Buddha's remains first, he had done so to let them do it at a time that suited them; as to not asking the Buddha to go on living, Māra had made him blind; and as to helping the Buddha's aunt and foster-mother Mahāpajāpati Gotamī/Mahāprajāpati Gautamī to become the first Buddhist friaress, he had thought of the Buddha's own debt of gratitude to her.

Especially interesting from our perspective, with some knowledge of 2500 years of later history, may be the two points where Ānanda had encouraged women in a way that didn't suit Indian society at his time. Of all participants of the council, he was the last to have become an *arahant*: only the very night before it began. On the other hand, he had lived very close to the Buddha more than any other friar. Might he perhaps have understood better than they the Buddha's way of regarding social matters?

All the texts collected by the first council were edited — orally and by heart — and became the first version of the two first parts of what would later become the *Tipiṭaka.* The popular language in North India was largely a number of Indo-Āryan dialects (Middle Indian or Prakrit; the Buddha very consciously did *not* make use of Sanskrit, which was the language of the intellectual élite). One may suppose that the Buddha had, during his wanderings, made use of different local dialects when teaching. To get some unity in the shape of the texts, a standard dialect was now created, and given the quite logical name 'text language' (*Pāli-Bhāsā*, later abbreviated to Pāli).

After the council and the rainy season, the friar Puraṇa came to Rājagaha, having not participated. The participants then told him what they had done, and asked him about his opinion. He answered that what had happened was very good, but as for himself, he would stick to the Buddha's teaching such as he had heard it himself from the Buddha's own lips.

This maybe can be taken to mean that even the council didn't have any absolute authority, and that the insight and understanding of individual man must never be subject to any central decrees.

The Second Council was held a hundred years later, and added some texts to the canon. At that time, only one of those friars who had personally met the Buddha was said to be still alive.

The life of the Buddha is the first fixed point in Indian history. After his death, there were extensive political upheavals in the subcontinent. The kingdom of Magadha annexed the republic of Vajji, and Kosala strengthened its grip on Sakya and some other small countries. Finally, Magadha engulfed Kosala. The Maurya Empire spread out over more and more of India. The Maurya king Candragupta converted to Jainism, abdicated, and spent the rest of his life as a Samaṇa. From the west came a Greek, and later Roman, influence. Alexander the Great reached north-western India during his campaigns. The first post-canonical Pāli text, the *Milindapañhā*, is a dialogue held in this region between the Buddhist friar Nāgasena and the Greek king Menandros (in English sometimes called Menander, in Pāli Milinda). The Greek and Roman influence would greatly affect the development of the Buddha image.

During these first centuries Buddhism was, same as the other Samaṇist schools, largely a free popular movement. That situation would be radically changed when Candragupta's grandson Asoka/Aśoka rose to power. Asoka had continued the military expansionist politics of his fathers, but he is said to have been so perplexed at an unusually gory battle that he suddenly became a pacifist. He converted to Buddhism, but unlike his grandfather, he didn't abdicate. He stayed on the throne and tried to rule in a Buddhistic spirit.

Many Buddhists are regarding Asoka's conversion as the great victory of Buddhism, but I'm not quite convinced about that. Admittedly, Buddhism grew in outer strenght during his time, but it was also subjected to state control; and as history has taught us, state control is always detrimental to any religion. Some descriptions in the *Tipiṭaka* of an ideal ruler, *cakkavattin/cakravartin*, probably intended to be read as a utopian ideal to strive for, as a moralizing yarn and not as literal historical truth, unfortunately has caused an exaggeratedly high appreciation of actually existing rulers who as a matter of fact were very far from realizing this ideal, from Asoka of India in ancient times to king Bhumibol of Thailand or king Sihanouk of Cambodia today. [A *cakkavattin* is, e.g., said to rule his country without any use of violence. As far as I know, no historically documented government has even tried that.]

Whatever you think of Asoka, however, you can't disregard his importance, both good and bad, for the history of Buddhism. The oldest written sources of Buddhism are his rock and pillar edicts, giving simple moral advice. These were always formulated in the local dialect (several kinds of Prakrit, plus a couple of texts in Greek and one in Aramaic). During his time, the Third Council assembled, finalized the edition of the Pāli *Tipiṭaka,* to the two first parts of which — the *Vinaya Piṭaka* and the *Sutta Piṭaka* — now had been added a third, the *Abhidhamma Piṭaka,* with advanced texts about Buddhist psychology. Last not least, he sent out friars to teach the *Dhamma* abroad, including the Middle East and the Balkan Peninsula; and this started the next great chapter in the propagation of Buddhism.

Buddhism in Asia: From Asoka to Olcott

Asoka sent his messengers in all directions. Those who went westwards probably reached the south-east corner of what we now call Europe, i.e., the Balkan Peninsula. It isn't even impossible that small groups of Buddhists had existed there already for a couple of generations, since the campaigns of Alexander. Buddhism didn't get any dominating position in the Eastern Mediterranean, though. The religious pluralism existing there in antiquity began to be gradually stifled, when the emperor Constantin converted to Christianity. Since then, questioning monotheism in those countries has not been conducive to good health and a long life, nor even to confess another kind of monotheism than the one which happens to be correct at a given moment. Gory show-downs have been common, from the battles between Christian Unitarians and Trinitarians in late antiquity to our days' Bosnia: Christians against Christians, Christians against Muslims, Muslims against Muslims. If any Buddhists have lived there, they have had a very good reason to keep a low profile.

Especially successful was the information given to Ceylon. That island, like the southern tip of the Indian mainland, did not belong to Asoka's empire. It was, at least formally, a sovereign country under king Devanampiya Tissa (which didn't mean, however, that Asoka didn't have some influence there). To the island Asoka sent his son Mahinda, who was a Buddhist friar. As has been mentioned already, Mahinda made the king renounce pleasure hunting and similar immoralities, and converted him to Buddhism.

According to official history, Buddhism didn't come to Ceylon until the king was converted; but that is probably true only if you hold the history of a country to be that of its rulers. Keeping in mind the close commercial connections between the island and the mainland, it is very likely that Buddhism had entered already at an earlier stage; especially as Buddhists, unlike the Brāhmaṇists of that time (and the most orthodox Hindus of ours) didn't have any taboo against travelling over 'black water', and therefore got an important position in India's foreign trade. Now, however, Buddhism became the state religion, and so it remained until the British in the nineteenth century colonized the last independent part of the inland. [On the other hand, that kingdom of Ceylon which became independent in 1948, and which in 1972 was transformed to the "Democratic Socialist Republic of Sri Lanka" (to keep that name under officially Pro-Socialist and Anti-Socialist governments alike), is formally a secular state, although a large majority of its population is regarding themselves as Buddhists.]

In Ceylon, Buddhism fairly soon became ethnically lopsided since almost only the Sinhalese majority embraced it, while the Tamil minority in the north remained Brāhmaṇist, and later Hindu. (The Muslims in Ceylon are largely Tamil-speaking, but they regard themselves as a proper ethnical group; unlike the Christians, especially Catholics, who exist since the Portuguese colonization among both Sinhalese and Tamils.) Confusion has been caused by the fact that Sinhalese friars started to write the country's verse chronicle (especially the *Mahāvaṁsa*, the writing of which is still not finished, as history isn't) not in Sinhalese but in the source language of Buddhism, in Pāli. In the first part of the chronicle, a few highly apocryphical stories were also included about alleged visits of the Buddha to Ceylon (not by one word mentioned in the *Tipiṭaka*), and in later parts there are extremely partial and prejudiced descriptions of early wars between Sinhalese and Tamils. Use was thus made of the holy language of Buddhism to propagate an Anti-Buddhist morality.

On the other hand, the island has played an important role for the survival of this language. In Ceylon assembled, some hundred years BC, the Fourth Buddhist Council (according to South Buddhist tradition), and at that occasion, the *Tipiṭaka* was actually written down for the first time (on palm leaves), having been learnt by heart for many generations.

About a thousand years after the Buddha, the friar Buddhaghosa came from India to Ceylon and became the most important author of post-canonical Pāli literature. He wrote a compendium of the teaching of Buddhism, titled the *Visuddhimagga*, 'Path of Purity'. He also was given access to the extensive commentaries in Sinhalese to the Pāli *Tipiṭaka*, and founded on those, he wrote a commentary in Pāli. It is not clear how much of his commentary was translations and how much was his own inventions, for the Sinhalese material has later been lost.

It is uncertain when Buddhism came to the region called in Pāli *Suvannabhūmi*, in Sanskrit *Suvarṇabhūmi*, meaning (same as the later Spanish name 'El Dorado' of another part of the world) 'Gold Country', i.e., the greater part of mainland South-East Asia. The present ethnical majorities of Burma and Siam (by their respective governments nowadays called Myanmar and Thailand) have been there for about one thousand years only. Before that however, the Mon people, now an oppressed minority in both countries, had a large realm in the region, and Buddhism probably was strong there already at that time.

In India, controversies among the friars about details in their disciplinary rules were by and by combined with a schism about the choice of language. When Asoka wrote his edicts, he kept to the Buddha's principle that the *Dhamma* should be presented in the listeners' own language, in North India thus normally in Prakrit — not Sanskrit. The oldest existing version of the Buddhist canon (*Tipiṭaka*) was, as has been mentioned, edited orally at the three first councils in India, in a form of Prakrit finally named Pāli, and was for the first time written down in the same language at the Fourth Council in Ceylon. One faction of the *saṁgha* — probably more or less the same one as wanted less strict disciplinary rules — thought, however, that Prakrit didn't have enough status, so they produced a Buddhist Sanskrit canon (*Tripiṭaka*). The greater part of the original of this version has been lost, but before it was, it was used as a foundation first of the Chinese *Tripiṭaka* (the first extensive Buddhist translation project, led by the Indian friar Kumārajīva, who had emigrated to China), and then of the Tibetan Kanjur. The Chinese canon was also to be used in Korea, Japan, and Annam (later called Vietnam), the Tibetan one in Mongolia and adjacent parts of Siberia, and finally by the Kalmucks in the European part of Russia.

The two versions of the *Tipiṭaka/Tripiṭaka* were to be the basis of the two main schools in the history of Buddhism: the Pāli-based *Theravāda*, 'Teaching of the Elders', and the Sanskrit-based *Mahāyāna*, 'Great Vehicle'.

A term with which you have to be careful is *Hīnayāna*, 'Inferior Vehicle'. (The somewhat nicer translation 'Small Vehicle' is doubtful. *Hīna* is a qualitative word. The corresponding quantitative one is *culla.*) That word originally referred to the earlier stages of the Buddhist Sanskrit tradition, but later it has, by the followers of *Mahāyāna*, been used quite unhistorically also about the Pāli Buddhists (with whom they probably didn't have any contact when the term was coined), and this wrong use of the term has unfortunately become quite common in Western books. Many *Mahāyāna* presentations of Buddhism, not least Tibetan ones, also confuse the concepts. When authors belonging to the Tibetan tradition compare there own school with *Hīnayāna*, one should therefore keep in mind that their description of the latter does not necessarily have any greater similarities to the historically existing *Theravāda* (even if they should happen to think so themselves). Sometimes, it seems doubtful whether information about *Hīnayāna* in *Mahāyāna* sources is referring to any historical realities at all, or whether the authors are polemizing against a theoretical model created by themselves.

The Pāli Buddhists in Ceylon and Burma were to support each other at several occasions, not least with ordination of friars when the *saṁgha* had a crisis in one of the two countries. Later, a similar collaboration was initiated between Ceylon and Siam. [The historical relations between Burma and Siam have been marked by a deep military and political enmity, more or less similar to the one between England and France in Europe, and with as little basis in Buddhism as the Hundred Years' War had in Christianity.] Pāli Buddhism also came to dominate in Laos (whose main language, Lao, is related to Thai and used by the people also in North-Eastern Siam) and Cambodia.

Buddhism was largely spread through commercial contacts. As has already been mentioned, Indian Buddhists had no taboo against travelling over 'black water', i.e., leave India, so they came to dominate India's foreign trade.

To the north-west, Buddhism went during the first one

thousand years after the Buddha at least to the Caspian Sea. There, Buddhists seem to have met merchants from even further north and west, for a small Buddha image, probably made in India, has been found at the island of Helgö close to present-day Stockholm, where it must have been brought during the Migration Age, several centuries before the beginning of the Viking Age. (The image is now at the Swedish Museum of National Antiquities in Stockholm.)

Nowhere did Buddhism get a monopoly, nor strived to get one. In India and Ceylon, Brāhmaṇism remained and was after sometime changed into Hinduism. In mainland India, Jainism as well continued to thrive. In South-East Asia, Buddhism co-existed with different kinds of Animism, in Tibet with its ancient indigenous Shamanism (*Bönpa*), in China, Korea, and Vietnam with Confucianism and Taoism, in Japan with Shinto. Perhaps especially the interaction of Buddhism and Taoism turned out to be very productive. In their oldest forms, the two teachings are closely related, although they probably arose independently of each other.

The relationship between Buddhism and Confucianism was more complicated. At times the two, plus Taoism, collaborated harmoniously; but Confucianism is — unlike Buddhism and Taoism — essentially authoritarian. During certain periods, when its position as state religion was very strong, Buddhism was persecuted.

The relationship between Buddhism and Shinto has oscillated in a similar way. Often they have lived together without any frictions; but the firm military tradition in the Japanese state, and in certain branches of Shinto, has sometimes coloured even local Buddhism, and hidden its original pacifism. Especially during the period from the Meiji Restauration in the nineteenth century to the end of World War II, State Shinto was very strong, and gave little space for other schools of thought.

In India, where Buddhism arose and has at times been strong, there was a gradual shift back to Brāhmaṇism. At the same time, the latter absorbed elements of Buddhism and Jainism, and when Islam came to India from this as well; and thus arose Hinduism. The position of Buddhism in its country of origin was weakened, due to external competition as well as internal decadence. A finish was made when the great Buddhist university of Nālandā was devastated, and some of its last teachers fled to Tibet. This happened at about the same time as the first European universities were founded in Bologna and Paris. The Nalanda University had then been active for about a thousand years.

When Buddhism expired in India, it lived on in the neighbouring countries. A crucial crisis arose there some centuries later, when the Portuguese rounded the Cape of Good Hope and started the European colonization of large parts of Asia.

One of Portugal's first Asian conquests was the coasts of Ceylon. After sometime, the Sinhalese king managed to throw the Portuguese out, but to do so he needed the help of the Dutch. A later king later saw a need to throw out the Dutch, this time with the help of the British; and the latter weren't god rid of very soon. On the contrary, they conquered in time *all* the island, thus making an end of the Sinhalese kingdom. The British also conquered mainland India, Burma, the Malacca peninsula and the northern part of Borneo. The French took Indochina, the Dutch the southern part of Borneo and the rest of Indonesia. Siam managed to keep its independence by exploiting its strategical position at the border between Britain's and France's empires, and by cultivating contacts with such European countries as were strong enough to support them, but weak enough not to be able to conquer them, e.g., Denmark and the other Scandinavian countries.

[This didn't prevent the country, though, from absorbing such Western ideas as suited its rulers. Its present lese-majesty law, among the hardest in the world, is *not* based on Buddhist ideas, nor in any way compatible with Buddhism, but built on the Christian thought of the 'Kingdom by Grace of God'. It was imported from England. According to Buddhism, a ruler should *welcome* criticism. If he doesn't, he is not competent to rule.]

Japan, too, remained independent, by isolating itself from the rest of the world during long periods. Europeans never managed to crack Tibet, but China got under a strong Western dominance.

In many places, the colonial powers made an effort to take over education, and the European churches exploited this fact in their try to crush the indigenous religions and replace them with their own.

Buddhism in the World: From Olcott to Today

The Pan-Asian era of Buddhism more or less started in Ceylon, So did its global period.

The Portuguese colonizers had been more interested in the local people's souls than in their skin-colour. If a Ceylonese —whether Sinhalese, Tamil or something else—was baptized, he had rather good chances to make a career. The Dutch and, especially, the British were more racist, so in this country, the Dutch Reformed Church as well as the Anglican one (though proudly calling itself 'Church of Ceylon'!) are still relatively small, while the Catholics have remained a significant minority.

On the other hand, the British were the first who managed to conquer the entire island, which caused a serious crisis for local traditions. For sure, even Christian locals were excluded from higher positions by their complexion, but the Buddhist school system was still subjected to hard pressures, while the Christian one was strongly supported by the colonial power.

Now it so happened that the Buddhist friar and orator Migettuwatta Gunananda challenged a number of Christian speakers to a series of public debates. The last of these was held in Panadura in 1873, and is known in the history of religions as the Panadura Controversy.

After the debate, the Buddhists regarded themselves as victors, and the Christians said as little of the matter as they possibly could. John Capper at the *Ceylon Times* published a book with English translations of contributions to the debate, and that book got a large circulation in Europe and North America.

It was read by, among others, Henry S. Olcott, a discharged colonel of the American North State Army who, after the end of the North American Civil War, had started the cultivation of more peaceful interests. In 1875 he founded, together with the Russian emigrant Helena Blavatsky, the Theosophical Society.

The role of Theosophy in the history of Buddhism is an ambivalent one. On one hand it has had a great importance in encouraging an interest in Buddhism, both in traditionally Buddhist areas and others. On the other hand, it has also encouraged confusion. It tends to mix Buddhist elements with Hindu and others, and unlike original Buddhism — the Buddha, as has been already said, refused flatly to make any difference whatsoever between an exoteric doctrine and an esoteric one (*anantaram abahiram*) — Theosophy has had a strong tendency to refer to 'secret', and thus uncheckupable, sources. A similar confusion is today being propagated by the so-called New Age movement.

May 17th 1880, Olcott and Blavatsky came to Ceylon, where they formally converted to Buddhism. They were probably the first Westerners in modern times to do so. Olcott would then live for long periods in Ceylon and India, and he made a great contribution to the restauration of the Buddhist school system. This angered the British, but today there is a statue of him outside the Central Station in Colombo, whose main street is called the Olcott Mawatha.

The visit of Olcott and Blavatsky made a deep impression on a sixteen-year-old boy named David Hewavitarne. He came from an old Buddhist family but had gone to Christian schools, with a lot of conflicts with the teachers about the exercising of his religion. Not long afterwards he began to live as a lay ascetic, under the name of Anagārika ('Homeless') Dharmapāla. (A formal friar's ordination he got just before his death in 1933.)

The Anagārika Dharmapāla now began to help Olcott bring new life to the interest of the Sinhalese in their own religion. At the age of nineteen, he was tempted to study the occult aspects of Theosophy, but Blavatsky herself discouraged him from that, and told him to concentrate instead on the oldest form of Buddhism and to study Pāli. At that time, in 1884, the Pāli texts had not yet been printed, so he had to find some old palm-leaf manuscripts to read them.

At a later stage, the Anagārika Dharmapāla also made a great contribution to the restauration of the classical places of Buddhist pilgrimage in North India. (His ashes are today in Sārnāth, where the Buddha once began to teach.) He also made several trips abroad and spread some knowledge about Buddhism in Europe and North America, e.g., by participating in the *Parliament of Religions* which was held in Chicago in 1893.

A text with great importance for the growing interest in Buddhism in the West was Edwin Arnold's epic poem 'Light of Asia', which is still being printed again and again. [External pressures forced Arnold, in order not to be regarded as a 'pagan', to write a corresponding epic about Jesus. It was named 'Light of the World' and is today totally forgotten.]

The canonical texts of Buddhism began to be translated into Western languages in the nineteenth century. First was the *Dhammapada*, translated from Pāli to Latin by the Danish indologist Fausboll. After that, most translations have been made into English, with German at the second place.

An important institution during the past century has been the Pali Text Society in England, publishing the canonical Pāli texts, and many post-canonical ones, both in English translations and in the Pāli original in Latin transliteration. [That was, ironically enough, the first script to be used for international editions of Pāli texts. In Asia, each country had used its own writing, and printed editions of Pāli texts in Asian writings were made only when the Pali Text Society had already begun its activities.]

In Burma, also under British rule, Buddhist values were also defended. There, the Fifth Buddhist Council according to Theravāda tradition assembled at about the same time as the development mentioned above started in Ceylon, in 1870 in Mandalay. The whole *Tipiṭaka* was cut into marble slabs, in Pāli with Burmese letters. Later, the same thing was done with the medieval commentaries.

With both Ceylon and Burma under British rule (as well as India, where Buddhism was then practically extinct but yet had once arosen), it was natural for Britain to be one of the first European countries where Buddhism took root. In 1905, a Buddhist bookshop was opened in London by J. R. Pain, who had been a soldier in Burma, and R. J. Jackson, who began to teach Buddhism from a soap-box in Speakers' Corner. In 1906, the two founded the *Buddhist Society of England*, later to be renamed *Buddhist Society of Great Britain and Ireland.* In 1908, the English born Buddhist friar Ānanda Metteyya came to London and joined the organization, which was dissolved shortly after his death in the twenties.

In 1891, the Anagārika Dharmapāla had founded the *Maha Bodhi Society*, in order to win back the places of Buddhist pilgrimage in India as well as to make Buddhism better known in the external world. In 1925, he came to London and started a British branch.

In the British Theosophical Society, a Buddhist study group was founded. It became independent from Theosophy in 1926, and adopted the name *Buddhist Lodge*, changed in 1943 to *Buddhist Society*. While the the *Maha Bodhi Society* in England was pure Theravādin, the *Buddhist Society* was open for all Buddhist schools. In practice, it was dominated by Zen.

In the sixties, the English Buddhist friar Saṅgharakṣita came back to London, after many years in India, and started a Buddhist activity in the East End and for the working classes; the earlier Buddhist organizations in England had been mainly upper and middle class oriented.

Today, Buddhism is an established minority religion in Britain, and so it is in Germany, which didn't have any colonies in the Buddhist world, but whose philosophers have often been critical to the dominating Christianity. [German pluralism was also strengthened by the fact that the country has never been really united, as well as by the fact that the Catholic and Lutheran churches have for a long time been about equal in strength, so no single church could claim to be representing the whole country.] Schopenhauer was interested in both Buddhism and Hinduism, and even Nietzsche was at times more positive to Buddhism than is usually imagined.

The German friar Nyanatiloka and his disciples, several of whom (especially Nyanaponika) were also German, were active in Ceylon during the inter- and post-War periods, making great contributions as authors and publishers. In the Weimar Republic, Buddhist activities were dominated by Paul Dahlke in Berlin and Georg Grimm in Bavaria. In the Third Reich,

Buddhism was forbidden — when Hitler finally was informed that there were some Buddhists in his country, which didn't happen until the beginning of the fourties. When Germany and Berlin were divided after the War, both Grimm's and Dahlke's centres happened to be in the Western zone and sector respectively, so they could continue their activities. In time, more and more Buddhist groups were founded, and Germany got Europe's first national Buddhist umbrella organization: the *Deutsche Buddhistische Union.* [As far as I know, it is still the only one that is really functioning, so when the *European Buddhist Union* was later founded as an umbrella organization of national umbrella organizations, that project was not quite realistic.]

France, too, got Buddhist groups quite early, and somewhat later, the same thing happened in most Western European countries.

In Communist Eastern Europe, the Buddhists kept a low profile. For a while, there was a Hungarian branch of the Maha Bodhi Society, but it was soon forced to liquidate. In Czechoslovakia, Buddhists could act openly during the Prague Spring in 1968, but its leaders emigrated after the Soviet invasion the same year. In Poland, the balance of power of that time between Catholic Church and Communist Party gave greater opportunities also for religious minorities; opportunities that actually may have diminished somewhat when Communism fell and the Catholic Church strengthened its power.

And Poland did have some old traditions. In Warsaw, there was a Buddhist temple already before World War I; but at that time, Poland was divided between Germany, Austria-Hungary and Russia, with Warsaw in the Russian zone. The temple was mainly meant to serve Siberian Buddhists who had, probably not quite voluntarily, been recruited to the Russian Army and sent to Poland (in accordance with the principle practised already by the Roman Empire, that soldiers from conquered territories should serve as far from home as possible).

How the situation in East and Central Europe will develop now is impossible to tell. Political freedom has increased after the fall of the Berlin wall, but so has economical turbulence. A failed experiment in materialism has been replaced by another experiment in materialism. After Communism came Consumerism, and it is difficult to say which is worse.

A certain confusion has resulted in Europe from the fact that some originally Buddhist organizations have been taken over by the Theosophists without changing their names, and that more or less Hindu or New Age-oriented organizations have made use of Buddhist names and concepts without understanding them. Something similar happened in the USA, when the beatnik generation (e.g., the authors Ginsberg and Kerouac) adopted some very much selected parts of Zen Buddhism and tried to combine them with drug addiction, quite against the most elementary Buddhist morality. And (when writing this) not very long ago, the international press could report about 'suicide in *Nirvana*' — in a rock-band so named, that is, but without any connection whatsoever to the actual *nibbāna/nirvāṇa* concept.

There are, however, serious Buddhist activities as well in the USA and Canada. Especially the North American West Coast has got a lot of East Asian immigrants. The most common Buddhist schools there are Shin and Zen, later also Tibetan.

In several Western countries, e.g. the Scandinavian ones, Buddhism is in a way the most indigenous religion. It may not by far have the largest numbers of official followers, and most of those there are may be Asian immigrants, but in many countries, Buddhism was already there when Buddhist immigrants started to come, not by any missionary initiatives from the traditional Buddhist heartland and not by earlier immigrations, but because people living in these countries and born here, or perhaps having immigrated from other non-Buddhist areas, got interested in it and brought it here. There is also a marked Buddhistic influence in several European literatures of the twentieth and late nineteenth centuries, either directly or by the mediation of Theosophy.

In the Buddhism of Europe, there is today a certain polarization between those Europeans who first brought Buddhism here, and those Buddhist immigrants who have later come from Asia. Many Asians don't understand that Buddhism is not identical with those external forms to which they grew accustomed in their native countries, and they may just look blank if anyone tries to start an inculturation discussion of the kind that is going on, e.g., in the Catholic church (and at least in Sri Lanka also among Anglicans) — in spite of the fact that adaptation to local cultures is an age-old Buddhist tradition in Asia, expressed in those formal differences between local customs which are so important to some Asians. In Europe it is not customary that, e.g., Ceylonese and Siamese friars live in the same temple, although both are following the Theravāda school. [As a comparison one could mention that Catholic immigrants in predominantly Protestant areas, such as Sweden, can sometimes have tenths of different nationalities in the same congregation.]

Another problem is the fact that the most enthusiastic Buddhists in the West often spend such a long time in Asia that sometimes they become more Asian than most Asians and alien to their own cultures (which is not a Buddhistic attitude at all). There are also Western Buddhists who have never been to Asia, but who still want to copy the external forms of some Asian country, being Exotists rather than Buddhists. This has especially furthered the spread of the Tibetan tradition in the West, which on one hand may give some hope of the survival of Tibetan culture in spite of China's genocidical occupation of

Tibet; but which, on the other hand, has indeed confused matters a lot. Many Tibetans, even some very learned Lamas, just can't distinguish between Buddhist and Shamanist elements in that mixed religion which they are practising, and it won't be easier for such Westerners as get their first knowledge about Buddhism through the Tibetan tradition.

Two other groups are Western Buddhists of the second and third generations, who are increasing, and immigrants or refugees from countries with no Buddhist tradition; for some people, their more or less forced departure seems in itself to create an understanding of Buddhism.

In the USA and Canada, the situation is a little different, as has already been mentioned, partly because of the large East Asian immigration, especially in the Western states and provinces (Hawaii, California, British Columbia) — the Japanese immigrants and their descendants got some problems after Pearl Harbor — and partly because first beatniks and then hippies adopted some isolated elements of Buddhism and combined them with other things, in clear violence of Buddhist ethics. To Latin America, especially Brazil, Buddhism has come largely through Japanese immigrants.

In connection with the official 2500 years jubilee of the Buddha's death (the date of which has probably been as miscalculated as the birth of Christ was as starting-point for Western chronology, but never mind), two things happened. The Sixth Council according to Theravāda tradition assembled in Rangoon, Burma, with a new scrutiny and editing of the canonical Pāli texts (still with oral tradition as one of the sources used). Also, the number of Buddhists in its country of origin, India, increased very suddenly, especially among the outcasts.

As has already been mentioned, Buddhism almost disappeared from what is now the territory of the Indian

Republic about one thousand years ago. When the Anagārika Dharmapāla began his work to restore the places of Buddhist pilgrimage in Majjhima Desa, these were owned by Hindus. In 1892, the Maha Bodhi Society installed its headquarters in Calcutta, then capital of Imperial India (although its emperor didn't live there but in the Buckingham Palace of London, as he also happened to be the British king).

Even if the shrines were repaired and did attract many foreign Buddhists, the Indian ones remained few (perhaps some hundred thousands) until 1956. Then it happened that the main author of the Indian Constitution, Bhimrāo Rāmjī (Bābāsāheb) Ambedkar, born Hindu but outcast, after many attempts gave up all hope of freeing Hinduism from the cast system, and in that year, he converted to Buddhism. A great number of outcasts followed his example, so the number of registered Buddhists in India was multiplied by ten in just some months, from some hundred thousands to a couple of millions.

Here it might be mentioned that even the Mahatma Gandhi wasn't interested in abolishing the caste system. He just wanted to soften it. It is said that when Gandhi got the idea to call the outcastes not 'untouchable' but, politically more correct, *harijan*, 'God's children', naughty Ambedkar asked him who, if God was father of outcasts, might be father of the Caste Hindus. . .

Ambedkar was born 14 April , 1893. He became Minister of Justice in the first government of independent India in 1947, but resigned in 1951. He died 6 December 1956, just a few months after having embraced Buddhism. This, together with the expected opposition of the Indian upper classes, made great problems to the new movement. Besides, this had received very little support from the old 'Buddhist' countries, where many were accusing them of working 'politically': a very interesting view, historically speaking, as the very thought that religion and politics could at all be separated has existed for only a couple of centuries, and is of Western origin to wit.

The Ambedkar movement has, however, got some support later from the organization of the already mentioned English friar Saṅgharakṣita, called the *Friends of the Western Buddhist Order*, as well as from the Bangkok based but, for being Siamese, relatively dissident *International Network of Engaged Buddhists.*

Today, the world's religious map is being redrawn from scratch. The extremist form of that principle formulated in the Peace Treaty of Westphalia: *cuius regio, eius et religio* — 'who rules the realm shall also chose the religion' — is hardly applied in any country nowadays, except possibly the Vatican City State (even countries expressly founded to serve the interests of a specific religion, such as Israel and Pakistan, have citizens of other religions than the state's official one), but it has stubbornly stayed in the atlases, where some areas have been marked as Buddhist, others as Christian, and still others as Muslim. The progress of communication technology, from stage-coaches and optical telegraphs to jet-flights, telefax, and internet, make this map more and more complicated. In many towns today it would have to mark each flat separately, and to be up-dated every time someone is moving.

But this has really always been the case. A man or a woman can be Buddhist, Christian, or Muslim. A country can't. Whenever a country has been said to be, the alleged unity has been upheld by force.

And when the map of religions is splitting up like a jig-saw puzzle, it turns out that there are Buddhists everywhere (although not all of them know it's called 'Buddhism'), and that nowhere true Buddhists are a majority (same as true Christians or true Muslims).

Glossary

Ajātasattu/Ajātaśatru : king of Magadha at the time of the Buddha, son of Bimbisāra (see that word); is said first to have tried to murder his father, unsuccessfully, then to have succeeded him after his abdication, and finally — according to post-canonical sources only — to have had him imprisoned and at last murdered.

Ambedkar, Bhimrāo Rāmjī (Bābāsāheb): activist for India's outcastes, main author of the Indian Constitution, wished (unlike Gandhi) not only to soften the caste system but to abolish it; converted to Buddhism a short time before his death in 1956, and several millions of outcastes followed his example.

Amida: Japanese form of Amitābha; see that word.

Amitābha: name of a non-historic Buddha in the *Mahāyāna* tradition, especially important in Shin (see that word).

Ānanda: a cousin of the Buddha's, and one of the foremost friars when he lived; served for many years as his personal assistant and learnt by heart a great number of his sermons, which became the foundation of the middle part of the *Tipiṭaka* (see that word).

Anāthapiṇḍika/Anāthapiṇḍada: one of the Buddha's foremost lay disciples; donated the estate of Jetavana near

Sāvatthī to the Buddhist community.

anattā/anātman: not-self, the teaching that man's mind doesn't contain an eternal and unchanging core; one of Buddhism's most fundamental concepts.

anicca/anitya: impermanence; one of Buddhism's most fundamental concepts.

Arahant/Arhant: a human being completely free from greed, hatred and delusion.

Arnold, Edwin: English nineteenth-century poet, author of the epic poem 'Light of Asia', which contributed greatly to Western interest in Buddhism.

Asoka/Aśoka: an emperor who first conquered his empire, encompassing most of the Indian mainland, and then converted to Buddhism; author of Buddhism's oldest written sources, the Aśokan Rock and Pillar Edicts; important for the propation of Buddhism outside India by sending Buddhist teachers abroad.

Aṭṭhakathā: medieval Pāli commentaries to the *Tipiṭaka*; much of it was written by Buddhaghoṣa at the basis of a commentary, now lost, in Old Sinhalese.

Benares Sermon: *Dhammacakkappavattanasutta*, the Buddha's first lecture, given to the five ascetics in present Sārnāth near Benares.

Bimbisāra: king of Magadha at the time of the Buddha, one of his lay disciples.

Blavatsky, Helena: together with Olcott (see that word) founder of the Theosophical Society (cf. Theosophy); is, on one hand, through the propagation of Theosophy, historically important for the spread of religious freedom, but has, on the other hand, created much confusion by the alleged relevations of her 'secret masters', the contents of which is very different from the teaching of Buddhism.

Bodh Gayā: the Hindu name of Buddha Gayā, see that word.

bodhi: enlightenment, awakening.

Bodhi dharma: an Indian Buddhist friar who emigrated to China and founded Ch'an, which later was in Japanese called Zen (see that word).

Bodhisatta/Bodhisattva: a future Buddha, especially one who has decided to become a *Sammasambuddha* (see that word). The *Bodhisatta* ideal can be found in all schools of Buddhism, not only in *Mahāyāna*, as is sometimes asserted.

Brāhmaṇa: a member of the hereditary priest caste in Brāhmaṇism, and later in Hinduism. The brāhmaṇas are generally regarded as the highest caste in these systems, but in north-eastern India at the time of the Buddha, this claim was opposed by the kṣatriyas (see that word).

Brāhmaṇism: an Old Indian religion built on the caste system, with the brāhmaṇa caste as hereditary priesthood and the Vedas as 'revealed' scripture. When Islam came to India, more than a thousand years after the Buddha, Hinduism arose from the meeting between Islam and Brāhmaṇism.

Buddha: 'enlightened' or 'awakened'. Cf. *Paccekabuddha*, *Sammasambuddha.*

Buddha Gayā: a place of Buddhist pilgrimage, outside the town of Gayā in the present Indian state of Bihar; here, Siddhattha Gotama is said to have become a Buddha.

Buddhaghosa: foremost of all medieval commentators of the canonical Pāli texts.

Ch'an: Chinese form of Zen (see that word).

Devadatta: a cousin of the Buddha's, the great traitor in Buddhist tradition, more or less as Judas Iscariot in the Christian one.

devas: according to classical Buddhist texts beings on a 'higher' plane than the human, meaning a more comfortable one. They may be long-lived but they cannot be immortal, and they are not necessarily wiser than we, for the simple reason that a comfortable life normally doesn't promote wisdom. It is often said that a *deva* can't become enlightened unless he dies as a *deva* and is born as a human. A Buddhist doesn't need to believe in *devas*, and shouldn't worship them. He could, though, if he happens to count on their existence, include them in his loving-kindness meditations and in his compassion. To translate the word '*deva*' by 'god' is, in Buddhist contexts, not quite good.

Dhamma/Dharma: a Pāli/Sanskrit word with a lot of different meanings, of which the most significant one for Buddhism is 'the (Buddhist) teaching'. In the phrase *sabbe dhammā anattā, sabbe dhamma* means 'all phenomena' or simply 'everything'.

Dharmapāla, Anagārika (David Hewavitarne): a Ceylonese Buddhist activist, 1864-1933. He started the campaign to restore the places of Buddhist pilgrimage in India, and he made great contributions to the Buddhist reawakening in Asia and to the knowledge of Buddhism in the West.

dukkha/duḥkha: 'unsatisfactoriness', the central concept in Buddhist philosophy. It is often translated by 'suffering' or 'pain', but these words have a much too narrow meaning and should be avoided, if not especially explained.

Gotama/Gautama: the Buddha's family name.

Hīnayāna, 'Inferior Vehicle' (often translated by 'Small Vehicle', but that should have been *Cullayāna* — *hīna* expresses quality rather than quantity): a term used in *Mahāyāna* (see that word) originally about some early, and now long since extinct, Sanskrit based Buddhist schools, and also about a virtual school of Buddhism which has probably existed only as an invented polemical model. The term is often used, absolutely wrongly, about the Pāli based Theravāda (see that word). What *Mahāyāna* sources say about *Hīnayāna* does not hold true about the Theravāda.

Hinduism: that religion which arose when Brāhmaṇism was confronted with Islam. In spite of certain superficial similarities, Hinduism is fundamentally quite distant from Buddhism. Buddhism isn't, and has never been, a branch of Hinduism, as many Hindus assert. Cf. Brāhmaṇism, Samaṇism.

Joasaf or Josafat: a Christian (ex) saint and the main character in a medieval legend which, when better scrutinized, turned out to be an adaptation of the story about the Buddha. The name is probably a distortion of *Bodhisatta* (see that word).

kamma/karma: a central concept in Buddhism, as well as in several other thought-systems of Indian origin. According to Buddhism, *kamma* is the wish lying behind every intentional action, and giving its mental stamp to the actor. Thus, Buddhism does not teach that unintentional acts make *kamma*. The word covers the causes only, not their effects — cf. *vipāka*.

Kanjur: the Tibetan version of Buddhism's canonical texts, encompassing translations from Sanskrit and later additions. Cf. *Tipiṭaka, Tripiṭaka, Tanjur.*

karma: the Sanskrit form of *kamma* (see that word).

karuṇā: compassion.

Kassapa/Kaśyapa: one of the foremost friars at the time of the Buddha, after whose death he convened the First Buddhist Council. Zen tradition regards him as the Buddha's successor, but the *Tipiṭaka* says that the Buddha expressly refused to appoint one.

khandhas/skandhas: the five components of the living being, especially of man: the body, the feelings, the perceptions, the wishes and the consciousnesses.

Khattiya/Kṣatriya: the warrior caste in Brāhmaṇism, and later in Hinduism. The Buddha was born into this caste, but he completely distanced himself from the caste system.

Kosala/Kośala: at the time of the Buddha a kingdom with its centre in the present Indian state of Uttar Pradesh.

Kumārajīva: an Indian Buddhist friar who emigrated to China and guided the great translation project of the *Tripiṭaka* from Sanskrit to Chinese.

Kusinara/Kuśinagara: a place of Buddhist pilgrimage, the place where the Buddha died, now in the neighbourhood of the town of Gorakhpur in the Indian state of Uttar Pradesh near the Nepalese border.

Lumbinī: a place of Buddhist pilgrimage, the place where the Buddha-to-be was born, now in Nepal near the Indian border.

Madhyama Deśa: the Sanskrit form of Majjhima Deśa, see that word.

Magadha: at the time of the Buddha a kingdom with its centre in the present Indian state of Bihar.

Mahāpajāpati Gotamī/Mahāprajāpatī Gautami: the Buddha's aunt and foster-mother, later the first Buddhist friaress.

Mahāyāna, 'Great Vehicle': that Buddhist school which was originally founded on the (now lost) Sanskrit version *av* the canonical texts, later on their (still preserved) translations to Chinese (in China, Japan, and Vietnam) and Tibetan (in Tibet, Nepal, Mongolia, and Siberia). Cf. *Hīnayāna, Theravāda.*

maitrī: the Sanskrit form of *metta*, see that word.

Majjhima Desa/Madhyama Deśa, 'Middle Country': the region where the Buddha lived and worked, more or less the present Indian states of Uttar Pradesh and Bihar plus the adjacent parts of Nepal.

Māyā: the Buddha's mother.

metta/ maitrī: the unselfish and unsensual love to all who live and breathe. Can be cultivated.

Milindapañhā: the oldest post-canonical Pāli text, a dialogue held in Bactria in north-western India between the Buddhist friar Nāgasena and the Greek king Menandros (in Pāli Milinda).

mudita: sympathetic joy.

nibbāna/nirvāṇa: perfect freedom from greed, hatred and delusion.

Olcott, Henry, S.: a colonel in the American North State Army during the civil war, in 1875 co-founder of the Theosophical Society (cf. Theosophy). In 1880, he and Blavatsky (see that word) came to Ceylon, where they formally converted to Buddhism, a step of great importance for the self-esteem of the country's Buddhists. Olcott also made great contributions to the Buddhist school system of the island.

Paccekabuddha/Pratyekabuddha: 'Private Buddha', a Buddha who is enlightened with no help from others at a time when the *Dhamma* is not known, but who does not 'set the Wheel of the *Dhamma* in motion'. Cf. *Sammasambuddha.*

Pāli: the form of Prakrit (see that word) used in the oldest version of Buddhism's canonical texts, in medieval commentaries to these, and in other later literature in the same tradition. Cf. Prakrit, Sanskrit.

Panadura Controversy: a debate in 1873 in Panadura, Ceylon, between the Buddhist friar Migettuwatta Gunananda and Christian opponents, ending in a clear victory for the Buddhist side; made Olcott (see that word) interested in visiting Ceylon, which was to become of great importance for the further history of Buddhism.

pañña/prajñā: liberating wisdom or insight.

Pasenadi/Prasenajit: king of Kosala at the time of the Buddha, one of his lay disciples.

prajñā: the Sanskrit form of *pañña* (see that word).

Prakrit: a group of Middle Indian languages, of which the most important one for Buddhism is Pāli — see that word.

Prasenajit: the Sanskrit form of Pasenadi (see that word).

Pratyekabuddha: the Sanskrit form of *Paccekabuddha*, see that word.

Rājagaha/Rājagr̥ha: at the time of the Buddha capital of Magadha.

revelations: something which Buddhism definitively councils us not to believe in even if we've had them ourselves, since they are very difficult to distinguish from our own projections, and even more if others claim to have had them.

Sakya/Śākya: the Buddha's clan and their land, probably very much dependent on Kosala (see that word).

samādhi: calm and deep concentration. Please note that *samādhi*, according to Buddhism, is not the final goal of training, but at best a tool to get there, and at worst a trap.

Samaṇism/Śramaṇism: a religious/philosophical movement in India at the time of the Buddha, consisting of a great number of different factions with actually very little in common except their opposition against Brāhmaṇism (see that word) and their rejection of the caste system and the Vedas. Buddhism arose within its framework.

Sammasambuddha/Samyaksambuddha: 'Rightly and Completely Awakened', a Buddha enlightened with no help from others at a time when the *Dhamma* is not known, and afterwards 'setting the Wheel of the *Dhamma* in motion', i.e., starting a Buddhistic teaching and founding a *saṁgha* and a *śāsana* (see those words). Cf. *Paccekabuddha.*

saṁskāra: the Sanskrit form of *sankhāra*, see that word.

samyaksambuddha: the Sanskrit form of *sammasambuddha* (see that word).

saṁgha: 'community' or 'fellowship'. Two specific meanings are especially important in Buddhism: *ariyasaṁgha*, 'community of noble ones', i.e., of people gone far enough to be at least *Sotapanna*s (see that word), and *bhikkhusaṁgha*, the community of friars.

sankhāra/saṁskāra: a Pāli and Sanskrit word with several meanings. In the phrases *sabbe sankhārā aniccā* and *sabbe sankhārā dukkhā, sabbe sankhārā* may be translated by 'all conditioned things' or 'all compounded things'.

Sanskrit: the Old Indian used as a learned language when the people were already speaking Middle Indian. The Buddha avoided the use of Sanskrit, because he wished to serve the people, but in later Buddhist traditions Sanskrit has often been used, often in a form influenced by later Indian languages and called 'Buddhist Hybrid Sanskrit'. Cf. Pāli, Vedic.

Sārnāth: a place of Buddhist pilgrimage, outside Benares, the place where the Buddha began his teaching.

Sāsana/ Śāsana: 'message', Buddhism as a historical fact. A *sāsana* has a beginning and an end, but the truth it does express (*Dhamma*, see that word) is, according to Buddhism, timeless.

Sāvatthī/Śrāvastī: at the time of the Buddha capital of Kosala.

Shin: an East Asian Buddhist tradition, primarily meant for those who are not capable of advanced meditation. By invoking the name of the Buddha Amitābha (see that word), one hopes to be reborn in his realm, the 'Pure Country', originally for being able there to continue one's way towards *nibbāna* under the best of circumstances; but the two concepts have often been confused in the later stages of this tradition. Cf. Zen.

Śramaṇism, see Sāmanism.

Śrāvastī: the Sanskrit form of Sāvatthī (see that word).

Siddhattha Gotama/Siddhārtha Gautama: the historical Buddha.

skandha: the Sanskrit form of *khandha* (see that word).

Sotapanna/Śrotapanna: 'Stream Enterer', one who has on his way towards *nibbāna* reached the point of no return.

Suddhodana/Śuddhodana: the Buddha's father.

Tanjur: commentaries to Kanjur (see that word).

Theosophy: an old term in the Western history of religions; in a more narrow meaning the name of the doctrine of the Theosophical Society, founded by Helena Blavatsky and Henry Olcott in 1875 (see the words Blavatsky and Olcott). This Theosophy has adopted some Buddhist thoughts and mixed them with Hindu and others and, not least, with Blavatskys own 'revelations'. Theosophy has, in spite of its vague thinking, been historically important for the progress of religious freedom in the West and for Buddhist reawakening in colonial Asia.

Theravāda, 'Teaching of the Elders': the Buddhist school founded on the Pāli version *av* the canonical texts; practised mostly in Ceylon, Burma, Siam, Laos, and Cambodia. Cf. *Hīnayāna, Mahāyāna*.

Tipiṭaka: the Pāli version of Buddhism's canonical texts, cf. *Tripiṭaka*.

Tripiṭaka: the Sanskrit version of Buddhism's canonical texts, probably younger than the Pāli version, although the language is more archaic. Most of the Buddhist Sanskrit canon has been lost in its original form, but translations of it had then already been the basis of the Chinese and Tibetan versions. Cf. *Kanjur, Tipiṭaka*.

upekkhā/upekṣā: equanimity, mental balance.

Vedic: the ancient Old Indian, cf. Sanskrit.

vipāka: the result of *kamma*, see that word.

vipassana/vipaśyana: 'clear·sight', Buddhist insight training.

Zen: a Chinese (Ch'an), Korean, Japanese and Vietnamese tradition, founded by the friar *Bodhidharma*, who emigrated from India to China about one thousand years after the Buddha. When *Bodhidharma* came to China, Buddhist activities there were very much text-oriented at the expense of meditation, and to restore the balance, he strongly emphasized meditation. When Zen has in our century been introduced in circles of a low intellectual level, such as most of the USA and much of Western Europe, this idea of a balance between text-study and meditation has been entirely lost, with sometimes disastrous results such as American 'Beat Zen' and similar anti-intellectual farces. Many Westerners think that Zen is identical with Japanese Buddhism, but that is wrong. In Japan, the Zen pracitioners have never been more than a small minority in comparison to other Buddhists. Cf. Shin.

Bibliography

[The amount of books about Buddhism in English is vast indeed, so I will just mention a few titles and publishers whom I feel to be most reliable.]

The canonical Pāli texts have been published several times. The classical edition is the one of the Pali Text Society, Britain, in Latin letters; the PTS has also published English translations of most canonical texts (I am not quite certain whether the last parts of the *Abhidhamma Piṭaka* translations have been published yet) and of several medieval commentaries (*aṭṭhakathā*). They are now working with the subcommentaries (*ṭīkā*).

A Royal Siamese edition of the Pāli *Tipiṭaka* (plus the oldest post-canonical Pāli text *Milindapañhā* and the *Jātakaṭṭhāvaṇṇanā*, Buddhaghosa's commentary to the Jātaka book of the *Tipiṭaka*, which in itself contains only verses and no prose), in Thai characters, was published in the 1920s and was donated to many libraries, where it may still be found.

A very good Pāli *Tipiṭaka* edition in Devanāgarī letters was published in the 1950s by the Nava Nālandā Mahāvihāra, India.

A publisher of great importance for the international knowledge of Buddhism is the Buddhist Publication Society in Sri Lanka. They publish both translations of canonical

Pāli texts (and some post-canonical ones) as well as books and booklets by contemporary authors. They specialize in the *Theravāda* school. The few *Mahāyāna* texts published by them are such ones that do not contradict the *Theravāda* view (which, however, is in itself by no means dogmatic.) Their catalogue (updated every year) may be sent for from Buddhist Publication Society, 54 Sangharaja Mawatha, P.O. Box 61, Kandy, Sri Lanka, phone and fax +94 -8-23679.

As to general introductions to Buddhism, a classical and well written one is the Ven. Walpola Rahula's *What the Buddha Taught*, published by Gordon Fraser, Britain (many editions—the first one in 1959). Other valuable books by the same author are *History of Buddhism in Ceylon* (1st edn. M. D. Gunasena, Colombo, 1956, 2nd edn. 1966) and *Bhikshuwage Urumaya* (2nd Sinhalese edn. Lankaputra, Colombo, 1948; English translation *The Heritage of the Bhikkhu*, New York, 1974). The latter book made me aware of the radical difference between the ethical ideas of the Buddha and those of the *Mahāvaṁsa*, a fact often forgotten by Sinhalese 'Buddhists' (whose opinion about Tamils is often more Mahāvaṁsist than Buddhist).

Speaking of Ethics, a good introduction to the subject is the Ven. H. Saddhatissa's *Buddhist Ethics: Essence of Buddhism*, Allen & Unwin, Britain, 1970.

Books about Buddhist meditation seem to be more popular than books about Buddhist ethics, which means that many readers wish to build, as it were, the upper floor of their house before the ground floor has even been planned. Books who teach meditation without morality may be mentally dangerous, and should be read — if at all — only in clear awareness of this fact.

Two meditation books, of many, who have been written with such an awareness, however, are Bhikkhu Khantipālo's *Calm and Insight: A Buddist Manual for Meditators*, Curzon Press, Britain, 1981; and Nyanaponika Thera's classical *The Heart of Buddhist Meditation*, 1st edn. Rider & Co., Britain, 1962 (reprinted several times). I find both to be highly recommendable.

Coming to the many existing biographies of the Buddha, there are two that I have found especially useful: Bhikkhu Ñāṇamoli's *The life of the Buddha*, Buddhist Publication Society, Sri Lanka, 1972, mainly compiled from the *Tipiṭaka* with some connecting texts by Ven. Ñāṇamoli himself (who also made all the translation from Pāli in the book); and K. D. P. Wickremesinghe's *The Biography of the Buddhā*, published by the author in Sri Lanka in 1972, more freely written but with footnotes mentioning the canonical and post-canonical texts from which he has received his information.

Index